Hellenism in Late Antiquity

JEROME LECTURES, EIGHTEEN

Hellenism
in Late Antiquity

THOMAS SPENCER JEROME LECTURES

G. W. Bowersock

Ann Arbor

THE UNIVERSITY OF MICHIGAN PRESS

Copyright © by The University of Michigan 1990
All rights reserved
Published in the United States of America by
The University of Michigan Press
Manufactured in the United States of America

1993   1992   1991   1990   4   3   2   1

Library of Congress Cataloging-in-Publication Data

Bowersock, G. W. (Glen Warren), 1936–
   Hellenism in Late Antiquity / G. W. Bowersock.
      p.   cm. — (Jerome lectures : 18th ser.)
   Includes bibliographical references.
   ISBN 0-472-09418-1 (alk. paper)
   1. Hellenism.   2. Christianity—Early church, ca. 30–600.
3. Paganism—Mediterranean Region—History.   I. Title.   II. Series.
DF240.B69 1990
292′.009182′2—dc20   89-20573
                                                                              CIP

Acknowledgments

According to the will of Thomas Spencer Jerome, the lectures he endowed are to be delivered both at the University of Michigan in Ann Arbor and at the American Academy in Rome. No lecturer could be assigned more agreeable settings than these. My fortnight in Ann Arbor in February of 1989 was the purest joy for me, as I savored the hospitality and learning of one of the great centers of classical studies in the world. The department's chairman, Ludwig Koenen, matched in the warmth of his welcome and the acuity of his observations the kind and perceptive treatment accorded to me by John H. D'Arms, dean of the Rackham Graduate School, who issued the original invitation to deliver the Jerome Lectures. The colleagues and students of these two scholars enriched my life in Ann Arbor beyond measure, and I think not only of the Department of Classics but equally of the Departments of History and Near Eastern Studies, and the program in Art and Archaeology. I must also mention for special thanks David Potter and Dean Homer Rose.

At Rome, in late April and early May of 1989, in the enchanting atmosphere of the American Academy, I enjoyed the wonderfully stimulating company of many friends from many countries. The Academy's director, Joseph Connors, was as helpful and encouraging throughout as Charles Babcock, who attended marvelously to every detail as professor-in-charge for Classical Studies. Their staff was a miracle of unobtrusive efficiency. I was also lucky enough to be at the Academy at the same time as my friends Herbert Bloch and Paul Zanker, from whom I never cease to learn and to draw inspiration.

Finally, I want to express my deep appreciation to Colin Day, director of the University of Michigan Press, which has been the publisher of the Jerome Lectures from the start. Dr. Day's steady support and accommodation in leading an inevitably fretting author to publication has meant more to me than he can realize.

26 June 1989   G. W. B.

Contents

Abbreviations

ADAJ	*Annual of the Department of Antiquities of Jordan*
BAR	*British Archaeological Reports*
BASP	*Bulletin of the American Society of Papyrologists*
BCH	*Bulletin de correspondance hellénique*
BMC Cat.	*Catalogue of the Coins in the British Museum*
CIS	*Corpus Inscriptionum Semiticarum*
CSCO	*Corpus Scriptorum Christianorum Orientalium*
FHG	*Fragmenta Historicorum Graecorum*
GRBS	*Greek, Roman and Byzantine Studies*
IEJ	*Israel Exploration Journal*
IG	*Inscriptiones Graecae*
JAOS	*Journal of the American Oriental Society*
JHS	*Journal of Hellenic Studies*
JRS	*Journal of Roman Studies*
PEQ	*Palestine Exploration Quarterly*
PG	*Patrologia Graeca*
REG	*Revue des études grecques*
SEG	*Supplementum Epigraphicum Graecum*
SIG³	*Sylloge Inscriptionum Graecarum* (3d ed.)
SNG, ANS	*Sylloge Nummorum Graecorum, Collection of the American Numismatic Society*
ZDMG	*Zeitschrift der Morgenländischen Gesellschaft*
ZPE	*Zeitschrift für Papyrologie und Epigraphik*

Prologue

Over many years, as I carried out more specialized work on the history of various parts of the eastern Mediterranean world in the Roman and early Byzantine empires, I came up repeatedly against the frustrating but obviously crucial problem of what Greek culture outside of Greece actually meant—in Asia Minor, in Syria, in Arabia, in Palestine, in Egypt. In all these places the Greek language and traditions adapted in some way to ancient and powerful indigenous cultures that were themselves subject to new pressures from Rome and later from the new Rome, Christian Constantinople.

The problem of Greek culture abroad has conventionally been cast in terms of Hellenization, which seems to imply the deliberate or inevitable imposition of Greek ways over local ones. Hellenization in this sense could be thoroughgoing or superficial, and by late antiquity most of it seemed to fall into the latter category. Yet Hellenism, by contrast, survived: for one thing it was a concept the ancients talked about, whereas Hellenization was not. Hellenism did not necessarily threaten local cultures, nor was it imperialistic. It seemed to me that Hellenization was a modern idea, reflecting modern forms of cultural domination.

Accordingly, I have tried to open up a new approach to Greek culture in the Christian empire, to determine why and how it survived as it did and why it was so regularly identified with paganism (despite the indignation of certain fathers of the Church). The study of late Hellenism reveals a pagan culture that is far from moribund. It is rather a living culture responding as sensitively to its Christian environment as Christianity itself responded to the pagan world in which it grew to maturity.

Paganism in late antiquity has invariably been described in terms that presuppose its gradual unimportance: *Untergang, Ausgang, la fin (du paganisme)*, twilight, and death, to name only a few well-known expressions. But this cannot be right. Discomfort has shown up in several places recently. Ramsay MacMullen, in an epilogue on "the manner of death of paganism," quotes Peter Brown with approval: "The historian of the late Roman church is in constant danger of taking the end of paganism for granted."[1] And Garth Fowden, in reviewing Robin Lane Fox's *Pagans and Christians*, which brings the subject more or less to the point at which my investigation of Hellenism begins, remarks perceptively, "Late paganism is still in urgent need of students, just to bring our understanding of its literary remains to the level already enjoyed by the patristic tradition."[2]

Hellenism provides, I believe, a unique instrument for putting this whole issue into a clearer perspective. It is gratifying to observe that Frank Clover and Stephen Humphreys, in their introductory remarks to a recent collection of valuable papers on late antiquity, seem to presuppose this view when they write, "Under Constantinople's aegis, the imperial Hellenism, decidedly Greek in form and outlook, replaced the old Graeco-Roman culture as the dominant way of life in the Roman Empire."[3] This is certainly true of the culture of the eastern Mediterranean, with which the present work is concerned. But I suspect that there are also important parallels to be sought in the West at the level of local culture.

---

1. R. MacMullen, *Paganism in the Roman Empire* (New Haven, 1981), p. 134.

2. G. Fowden, *JRS* 78 (1988): 173.

3. F. M. Clover and R. S. Humphreys, *Tradition and Innovation in Late Antiquity* (Madison, Wis., 1989), p. 10.

I

Paganism and Greek Culture

On March 1, 1843, a certain Dr. Tattam deposited in the British Museum some manuscript pages that he had acquired from a monastery in the Wadi Natrûn in Egypt. The pages were in quarto size and written in Syriac in two columns each. Further depositions from the same manuscript through the generosity of another collector in 1847 and 1850 brought the total of pages to 159 and revealed the author of the work they contained. He was none other than John, bishop of Ephesus in the sixth century A.D., and this was the third part of his *Ecclesiastical History*. The new text was presented to the world for the first time since the Middle Ages in an austere edition prepared by William Cureton, Canon of Westminster.[1]

John of Ephesus had long been known through other sources as a vigorous proselytizer and an immodestly self-promoting chronicler of his conversions of the heathen. But nonetheless the magnitude of the problems confronting this zealous missionary, as they appeared in his own account, surpassed all expectation. John went to convert the pagans of Asia Minor, in Lydia, Phrygia, and Caria, in 542, after repeated though frequently ignored temple closings and imperial interdicts.[2] John's mission to Asia came well after Justinian's attempt to repress the philosophical schools at Athens, a move which had led to the unseemly and abortive journey of the Athenian Neoplatonists to Persia to find inspiration and support from the Sassanian king.[3]

The first commentator on the new text of John, a Dutch Protestant living in England and writing in German, simply refused to confront the degree of exaggeration in John's narrative, but of the presence of some exaggeration he

---

1. W. Cureton, ed., *The Third Part of the Ecclesiastical History of John of Ephesus* (Oxford, 1853). The preface to this work contains an account of the acquisition of the manuscript.

2. For John in Asia Minor, see the most recent edition of the surviving text of *Hist. Eccles.* 3.3.36, CSCO vol. 106, Scrip. Syri 55:169 (Syriac). On imperial prohibitions of paganism, see the comprehensive survey by P. Chuvin, *Chronicle of the Last Pagans* (Harvard, 1990).

3. On Justinian's repression of education, see, for example, the judicious remarks of Averil Cameron, *Procopius* (Berkeley, 1985), p. 22.

evidently had no doubt.[4] John appeared to bear witness to a surprisingly vigorous paganism in Asia Minor over three centuries after Constantine had seen whatever it was that he saw (in the sky or in a dream) before the battle at the Milvian Bridge.

Writing of himself in the third person, John says that he began his mission in the mountains of Tralles, an important city in the Maeander valley that is still today an important Turkish town under the name of Aydın. The whole Maeander valley had been a region of extensive Greek settlement and culture for over a millennium. It was also a region of many small villages and towns scattered throughout the mountains that enclosed the valley on the north and south. Asia Minor had been famous for its urbanization in antiquity. As many as five hundred cities were said to have flourished there. John reported that he discovered many thousands of pagans in the mountainous territory above Tralles, and in one particular town high up in the mountains he found a famous temple of idolaters that had jurisdiction over some fifteen hundred other dependent shrines in the adjacent territories. The old men whom John met there told him that priestly representatives from the other shrines came together to this mountainous place every year in order "to learn," in the words of John, and "to receive the law" as to how they should carry out their priestly duties.[5] At this point the Syriac text uses the Greek word *nomos*, by now well embedded in the Syriac language but nonetheless probably reflecting the conversations that John must have had with the local inhabitants in their dialect of Greek.

Fifteen hundred pagan shrines, thousands of worshippers, and annual convocations at a sacred place high in the mountains all suggest that the pagan cults of the region were hardly on the wane. Although the new testimony of John of Ephesus surfaced in the nineteenth century, it remains today an invitation to reassess paganism in late antiquity. In the Maeander valley alone, still one of the most numinous landscapes in modern Turkey, there were clear signs that the old gods were alive and well. Near Magnesia a cult of Apollo that included a sacred cave and an ancient image of the god can be traced from the days of Darius the Great in the sixth century B.C. to the early sixth century A.D., over a thousand years later. The cult included some sacred gardeners, who planted trees in honor of Apollo and then, from time to time, in a fit of wild enthusiasm, would tear them out by the roots and carry them around in frenzy. These gardeners are already mentioned by Darius in a well-known inscription from the sixth century B.C., and they can

---

4. J. P. N. Land, *Johannes, Bischof von Ephesos: Der erste syrische Kirchenhistoriker* (Leyden, 1856), p. 60: "In wie weit diese Angabe übertrieben, lassen wir dahingestellt sein."

5. John Eph., loc. cit. (n. 2 above).

be seen depicted on the coins of Magnesia as late as the third century A.D. The Greek traveler Pausanias described the cult in the second century A.D.[6]

What is most remarkable is that the cult was known to the Neoplatonists at the end of the fifth century and the beginning of the sixth A.D. A famous pagan philosopher and doctor from Alexandria in Egypt visited this shrine, according to the testimony of Damascius.[7] He then traveled from there to the great city of Aphrodisias further to the east in the hills south of the Maeander valley. This eminent Alexandrian, Asclepiodotus, is known to have resided for a time at Aphrodisias and to have participated in what was obviously a thriving pagan society in the city. Asclepiodotus married the daughter of one of the most eminent members of the local council, a man who coincidentally happened to have the same name, Asclepiodotus, and who is commemorated in three epigrams to have survived on the site.[8]

In an important Syriac life of Severus of Antioch, the hagiographer Zacharias marvelously calls up the religious atmosphere of late antique Aphrodisias when he reports the appeals of a new Christian convert to his pagan brothers there. "Do you remember," he said to them, "how many sacrifices we offered together as pagans in Caria to the gods of the pagans when we asked them—these alleged gods, while dissecting their livers and examining them by magic—to teach us if we would succeed in conquering the Emperor Zeno? We received a multitude of oracles as well as promises at that time—how the Emperor Zeno could not resist, that the moment had come when Christianity would collapse and disappear and when pagan worship would take over again."[9]

Elsewhere in Asia Minor in the sixth century there were temples to Artemis and to Iphigeneia at Comana, according to the testimony of the historian Procopius.[10] Nor was the worship of sacred trees confined to Magnesia. John of Ephesus himself reports that, in overturning the altars

---

6. L. Robert, "Le dendrophore de Magnésie," BCH 101 (1977): 77–88, reprinted in Documents d'Asie Mineure (Paris, 1987), pp. 35–46.

7. Damascius Vit. Isid. p. 156 Zintzen, excerpt 117 from Photius. Cf. L. Robert, op. cit. (n. 6 above), on the identification of the toponym Ἀπόλλωνος Αὐλαί.

8. L. Robert, "Deux Épigrammes d'Aphrodisias de Carie et Asklépiodotos," Hellenica 4 (1948): 115–26 with Hellenica 13 (1965): 170–71. See also C. Roueché, Aphrodisias in Late Antiquity (London, 1989), pp. 85–93. Kenan Erim, director of the excavations at Aphrodisias, generously informs me that a cache of late Alexandrian bronze coins has been discovered behind the theater. Furthermore, near the Sebasteion he has uncovered a building that is clearly a late antique philosophical school (with busts of its teachers and tondo portraits of the great figures of the past—Pythagoras, Apollonius [of Tyana presumably], Socrates, Pindar). This important archaeological evidence will be published by R. R. R. Smith.

9. Zacharias Vit. Severi, in Kugener, Patrologia Orientalis 2.1 (1904), pp. 40–41.

10. Procopius Wars 1.17.11–12.

that had been defiled by the blood of sacrifices offered to pagan divinities, he brought down numerous trees that the local people worshipped. Further to the south in Lycia a cypress was thought to contain the spirit of an idol, and on the southern coast of Turkey there was another famous cult of Artemis, Artemis Eleuthera.[11] John of Ephesus was moving in a world of flourishing cults of great antiquity that represented at one and the same time local traditions, local cult objects, such as trees or idols, and a mythology that was Greek mediated by a language that was also Greek (if not of the purest). The indigenous languages, such as Phrygian, had long gone, but the indigenous cults remained, and they remained in Greek vestments.[12]

The religious world to which John of Ephesus gives us such sudden and startling access was no different in other parts of what had been the eastern empire of Rome and was now the new empire of Byzantium, itself the new Rome. In southern Syria a local god by the name of Theandrites bore in his own name a theological problem that the Christians thought they had created themselves. Theandrites means quite simply "The God-Man." His cult can be traced back for centuries in the fertile plain of the Ḥawrân, and his devotees can be found as far afield as North Africa, where Arab soldiers kept alive the cults of their homeland.[13] But Theandrites was not only a local god, he was international too. The great Neoplatonist teacher Proclus is said to have worshipped him in Athens.[14]

If the twentieth century has brought us no literary text quite so arresting in its revelation of late antique paganism as that of John of Ephesus in the nineteenth century, we can nonetheless evoke an equally astonishing discovery from the visual arts. Just six years ago the Polish excavators at the town of New Paphos on the island of Cyprus unearthed a group of mosaics that both illuminate and symbolize the powerful role of Dionysus in the Greek world of late antiquity.[15] Hitherto the most lavish proof of the potency of this great god of frenzy and intoxication had been the enormous epic poem from the fifth century A.D. by Nonnos of Panopolis in Egypt. This work, which survives in its entirety, runs to forty-eight books and is thus equal in

---

11. Cf. the discussions in F. R. Trombley, "Paganism in the Greek World at the End of Antiquity," *Harv. Theol. Rev.* 78 (1985): 334, and L. Robert, "Villes et Monnaies de Lycie," *Hellenica* 10 (1955): 197–99.

12. Trombley, op. cit. (n. 11 above), p. 336.

13. Damascius *Vit. Isid.* p. 272 Zintzen, excerpt 198 from Photius. Cf. L. Robert, *REG* 49 (1936): 1–6 (Volubilis), reprinted in *Opera Minora Selecta* 2.939–44. See also G. W. Bowersock, "An Arabian Trinity," *Harv. Theol. Rev.* 79 (1986): 21.

14. Marinus *Vit. Procli* 19.480, p. 76 Masullo.

15. W. A. Daszewski, *Dionysos der Erlöser*, Trierer Beiträge zur Altertumskunde, vol. 2 (Mainz, 1985).

size to the *Iliad* and the *Odyssey* combined. It is heavy going in Greek (or in translation, for that matter), composed as it is in a dense and allusive style with many references to obscure myths and gods. It is hardly surprising that it has not received the attention it deserves for our understanding of the paganism of late antiquity. The great new mosaics from New Paphos give us, by contrast, a Dionysus that is much more immediate. Nonnos's poem is part of a far greater historical fabric. (*PLATES 1–4.*)

In Egypt, the homeland of Nonnos, some of the most important texts from the Egyptian religious tradition, texts which were associated with the revelations of Hermes Trismegistos, Thrice-Greatest Hermes—texts which were alleged to be of immemorial antiquity in the region—circulated widely in Greek translation. The name of the Greek god Hermes was adapted to his Egyptian counterpart. The Hermetic doctrines came to acquire wide currency in pagan circles both inside and outside Egypt. But in a brilliant study of the Egyptian Hermes, Garth Fowden has rightly emphasized that, although the Egyptian milieu of the Hermetic writings had been long and irreversibly Hellenized in its language and thought patterns, it had never been turned into a Greek milieu.[16] Greek was the language and culture of transmission and communication. It served, in other words, as a vehicle. What happened in Egypt was not essentially different from the role of Greek and Greek mythology in giving expression to the cults of trees and caves in Asia Minor or to the cults of a god-man in southern Syria.

The significance of Greek culture in local paganism throughout the countries of the eastern Mediterranean has never been easy to make out. It has often been observed that Egyptian religion remained steadfastly Egyptian despite the Hellenic veneer (as it seemed), but it was not only in Egypt that local cults remained essentially what they were. The Arabian god at Petra, Syrian Bel, and the tree cults of Asia Minor were no more Hellenized than the cults of Egypt. Indeed the tenacity of paganism in Asia Minor, as John of Ephesus saw it, has sometimes been ascribed to the deterioration of the Greek language into impenetrable dialects that preserved the independence of their speakers from the central Christian administration.[17] But interpretations along these lines are both too simple and misconceived.

Part of the problem lies in the traditional emphasis in writings from the Renaissance to the present on the role of Greek language and philosophy in early Christianity. Intimations of Neoplatonism in the fathers and vestiges of pagan rituals in Christian worship, such as the cult of saints as an evolution

---

16. G. Fowden, *The Egyptian Hermes* (Cambridge, 1986), pp. 43–44.
17. Cf. Trombley, op. cit. (n. 11 above), p. 336.

of the cults of heroes and emperors, have been scrupulously disengaged and illuminated. But paganism itself, seen on its own terms not so much as a rival of Christianity but rather as a contemporary alternative expression of piety, remains relatively obscure. Paganism as a rival to Christianity was essentially a Christian perception. For the pagans, coexistence with another cult, however popular it might be, was always a real possibility. The priests at the pagan shrines of Asia Minor or Syria or Egypt hardly saw themselves in contention with the pope, and few of them even had the relatively modest ambitions of a Symmachus in trying to place a sacred emblem in a public place.[18]

In the three centuries from the conversion of Constantine to the Islamic conquest only the Emperor Julian ever seriously conceived of paganism in opposition to Christianity. And the reason for this is obvious, although it is rarely stated: Julian was raised as a Christian. He turned to paganism with the zeal of a convert, and his view of paganism was conditioned by his Christian upbringing. He was the sort of pagan that Christians conjured up. He, and he alone of all the eminent pagans of late antiquity, wanted to turn paganism into the very thing that the Christians most feared and fought. It is highly unlikely that he would ever have nourished such a desire had he been a pagan from birth.

The reason for these sharply differing conceptions of paganism on the part of Christians and the pagans themselves is that paganism was not (and never was) a church. Polytheism is by definition tolerant and accommodating. Although some cults might be officially adopted by a state, as at Rome, local cults throughout the provinces went their own ways on their own terms. In the territories where Greek was known to a greater or lesser extent from the time of Alexander the Great, if not before, local deities became more comprehensible and more widely known through an assimilation with Greek deities. But there was never a pagan church. Only Julian ever had the mad idea of trying to establish one.

The persistence of all these local traditions has suggested that there was no more than a superficial Hellenization in much of Asia Minor, the Near East, and Egypt. A truer or at least less superficial kind of Hellenization was sought in those great cities that displayed patterns of Greek town-planning with agoras and theaters, and especially Greek institutions such as agonistic competitions of athletes, musicians, and poets.[19] But even this criterion has

---

18. On Symmachus and the Altar of Victory, see the commemorative essays in F. Paschoud, ed., *Colloque genevois sur Symmaque à l'occasion du mille six centième anniversaire du conflit de l'autel de la Victoire* (Paris, 1986).

19. Cf. L. Robert, "Discours d'ouverture," Πρακτικά, Acta of the Epigraphical Congress at Athens in October 1982 (Athens, 1984), pp. 35–45.

turned out to be a deception. Cities that seemed to show all the external trappings of Greek urbanism have been shown to contain within them indigenous forms of urbanization that come into view long before any conquests at the hands of Arabs or Turks.[20]

The problem lies in the very notion of Hellenization. It is a useless barometer for assessing Greek culture. There is not even a word for it in classical or Byzantine Greek. Hellenism was a language and culture in which peoples of the most diverse kind could participate. That is exactly what makes it so remarkable. To say that cities such as Tralles or Gerasa were only superficially Hellenized is not helpful, if this is supposed to mean that those cities retained considerable local character; and it is hard to think of what else it could mean. Hellenism, which is a genuine Greek word for Greek culture (*Hellênismos*), represented language, thought, mythology, and images that constituted an extraordinarily flexible medium of both cultural and religious expression. It was a medium not necessarily antithetical to local or indigenous traditions. On the contrary, it provided a new and more eloquent way of giving voice to them.

The relation of Greek culture or Hellenism to paganism in late antiquity can be understood perhaps more clearly if we look at some examples of what was happening before the radiance of state-supported Christianity endangers the clarity of our vision. It has sometimes been said that Zenobia, the queen of Palmyra in the third century A.D., presided over a city and, for a while, an empire, that was not really Hellenic. This view found support in the ultimate struggle of Zenobia's career, in which she fought against a Roman emperor who appeared to stand for the traditional values of the Graeco-Roman world. Palmyra itself seemed not to be a truly Greek city because it lacked a theater, although it did have an agora and a *bouleutêrion* for the council; above all, it lacked athletic, musical, and poetic competitions. And yet, as anyone who studies the inscriptions of the city can readily ascertain, Hellenism lay at the very center of Zenobia's cultural world.[21] Palmyra was a bilingual city, and its inscriptions are not only balanced between Palmyrene Aramaic and Greek: it is clear that Greek influenced Palmyrene in its diction rather more than Palmyrene Greek. The columns, the architecture, the reliefs, and the funerary portraits that abound in the physical remains of Palmyra show throughout a strong Hellenic influence.

Zenobia herself gathered around her in the sumptuous buildings of her oasis city one of the most luminous collections of Greek intellectuals ever to

---

20. H. Kennedy, "From Polis to Madina: Urban Change in Late Antique and Early Islamic Syria," *Past and Present* 106–9 (1985): 3–27.

21. Cf. G. W. Bowersock, "The Hellenism of Zenobia," in *Greek Connections*, ed. J. T. A. Koumoulides (Notre Dame, 1987), pp. 19–27.

adorn an ancient salon. Longinus (possibly the author of the superb literary treatise *On the Sublime*), the orator Callinicus, and the Christian Paul from Samosata bear witness to genuinely Hellenic tastes. What is perhaps most revealing about Zenobia and her culture is the way it was perceived by the Graeco-Roman world and by the Arab world, to which she obviously belonged. From the Graeco-Roman side she was another in the long line of usurpers, trying to win power from the established authority. The Emperor Aurelian fought her as a rival, not as a barbarian, and after her defeat she was comfortably set up in the suburbs outside Rome and honored for the rest of her days. More revealing still is the Arab tradition as we know it through Arabic texts of the Middle Ages.[22] It is clear that Zenobia was not seen as a traitor to her people or as someone who had turned Greek. Her struggle was presented as a kind of civil war among the Arab tribes of the region—a civil war in which Aurelian took one side rather than the other. That Zenobia could be a Roman to the Romans and an Arab to the Arabs can only be explained by the miraculous refracting power of Hellenism.

Further south, in the province of Arabia, we can see in visual terms the adaptation of Hellenism to local culture through a remarkable sequence of Arabian coins that runs from the time of the Nabataean kings, who ruled the region before the Romans, down to the middle of the third century A.D. (*PLATES 5–8.*) The chief god of the Nabataeans, Dusares, had traditionally been worshipped in aniconic form, represented in carvings and in freestanding idols.[23] But Greek religion was, of course, anthropomorphic. The collision of Hellenism and the Nabataeans in Arabia allowed the visual language of the Greeks to give new expression to the native Nabataean traditions without in any way annihilating them. In some coins the original aniconic form of the great god Dusares can be seen standing flanked by two other nonrepresentational idols—his colleagues in a divine trinity.[24] This ancient aniconic form of the god appears on coins from the second and third centuries A.D., and yet at the same time in the same region the god is represented in Greek terms as a man. The anthropomorphism may be Greek, but the man most certainly is not. It is a Nabataean face that we see with a Nabataean coiffure. The face is the traditional image of Nabataean kings, as the coins show. It would have been comprehensible and inspiring in that form to the people of Arabia. In other words, Hellenism may have given the

22. M. Piotrovskii, "Arabskaya Versiya Istorii Tsaritsy Zenobii (Az-Zabby)," *Palestinskii Sbornik* 21 (1970): 170–83.

23. G. W. Bowersock, "The Cult and Representation of Dusares in Roman Arabia," in *Petra Symposium on the Caravan Cities* (Amman, forthcoming).

24. E.g., *SNG, ANS,* 6, nos. 1215 and 1253.

face to a god formerly worshipped as an idol, but its face was a local face. In one remarkable coin the god as a man can be seen confronting the god as an idol.[25]

These coins were issued in the capital city of the province, Bostra, now in southern Syria. This is a city that had a theater and the Greek institution of agonistic games. But the games were named in honor of the local deity, Dusares, while at the same time joining many other cities of the East in commemorating Augustus's victory at the Battle of Actium. Hence the name *Actia Dusaria*.[26] The double name that is both Hellenic and Semitic is an institutional and verbal analogue to the twofold representation of the god on the coins of the city. Are we to say that Bostra is any more Greek or Hellenic than Palmyra simply because these games were held there, when they were not at Palmyra? The games do not by any means represent a deepened or truer Hellenism. What they do indicate is status, status both within the province and within the empire itself. It is no accident that they were bestowed upon the city by Philip, the first Arab to sit upon the throne of the Caesars.

These examples from the third century, on the eve of the period we know as late antiquity, demonstrate clearly without any distraction from Christianity what Greek culture meant in the pagan life of the eastern Mediterranean. In language, myth, and image it provided the means for a more articulate and a more universally comprehensible expression of local traditions. This became the precious mission and character of Hellenism in the Christian empire of late antiquity. It is for this reason that the word Hellenism (*Hellênismos*) takes on a new meaning in late antiquity, a meaning that proclaims in the most eloquent way possible the relation between paganism and Greek culture. For Hellenism comes to mean "paganism" itself. The dictionaries and lexica have long recognized that *Hellênismos* in later Greek sometimes means paganism and sometimes Greek culture (or Hellenism as we use the word), and that *Hellênes* are sometimes "pagans" and sometimes simply "Greeks." Similarly the adjective *Hellênikos* sometimes means "pa-

---

25. Anthropomorphic Dusares: A. Kindler, *The Coinage of Bostra* (Warminster, 1983), cat. no. 18; *SNG, ANS,* 6, no. 1206. Nabataean royal faces: *SNG, ANS,* 6, no. 1440. Human form and idol: M. Rosenberger, *The Coinage of Eastern Palestine* (Jerusalem, 1978), Characmoba no. 2; A. Spijkerman, *The Coins of the Decapolis and Provincia Arabia* (Jerusalem, 1978), pp. 110–11, no. 5; *BMC Cat.* Arabia, p. 27, no. 3; Glendinning auction catalog of March 10, 1965, no. 180 with pl. 6, no. 180, from which the photograph on pl. 8 in the present book was made.

26. G. W. Bowersock, *Roman Arabia* (Harvard, 1983), p. 122 with n. 50, and "Greek Culture at Petra and Bostra in the Third Century A.D.," *Proc. of Delphi Symposium on Hellenism in the Near East*, European Cultural Center of Delphi, forthcoming.

gan" and sometimes "Greek."[27] The dual sense of these words lies at the heart of the present enquiry. Since paganism and Greek culture are patently not the same thing, the consequences of their being designated by the same word were obviously momentous. This was particularly true for those Christians who were busy writing and praying in Greek.

The use of Hellenic or *Hellênikos* in the sense of "pagan" seems to coincide with the beginning of late antiquity, if we understand that to be the Constantinian age. It is obviously a response to the increasing visibility and strength of the Christians, and it seems as if the first to use Hellenic in its religious sense were the pagans themselves. The earliest clear instances come from letters addressed to the Neoplatonic philosopher Iamblichus at the beginning of the fourth century.[28] They seem to reflect a desire for heightened self-consciousness and brotherhood among those who espoused pagan doctrines. But the word and its cognates swiftly appear in the new sense among the Christian writers. It surfaces already in Eusebius's *Life of Constantine*: *hellênizein* had meant—and in some writers, like Libanius, continued to mean—"to live as a Greek," "to be civilized in the Greek way," or simply "to speak Greek," but Eusebius employs it transparently in the sense of "to practice paganism."[29] Athanasius adroitly stigmatizes the Arians by labeling them "Greeks," clearly again in the sense of "pagans."[30] At the same time Eunapius in his *Lives of the Sophists* can write of a militant fourth-century pagan, who loved sacrificing (*philothutês*) as exceptionally Greek, manifestly in the sense of very much a pagan.[31] And indeed Eunapius glosses his remark by commenting that at the time the general movement of religious sentiment was going against paganism.

One might well wonder what word the Christians used for pagans before *Hellênikos* became the standard term, and that means specifically what the pagans were called in Christian writers before the fourth century A.D. Again the lexica and dictionaries are perfectly clear on this point, although its significance has not been much appreciated. In the Shepherd of Hermas, in Hippolytus, in Clement, in Origen, and elsewhere, the standard word for "pagan" is *ethnikos*, and the equivalent of *Hellênismos* in late antiquity is

---

27. Cf. I. Rochow, "Zu einigen oppositionellen religiösen Strömungen," in *Byzanz im 7. Jahrhundert*, Berliner Byzantinistische Arbeiten, vol. 48 (Berlin, 1978), pp. 227–29. See also the references in A. Kurmann, *Gregor von Nazianz: Oratio 4 gegen Julian—Ein Kommentar*, Schweiz. Beiträge zur Altertumswiss., vol. 19 (Basel, 1988), p. 110 (*ad* 30.19).

28. The references are collected in W. Koch's excursus on ὁ Ἑλληνισμός in *Rev. belge de phil. et d'hist.* 7 (1928): 539.

29. Euseb. *Vit. Const.* 2.44. Cf., for Libanius, A. J. Festugière, *Antioche païenne et chrétienne* (Paris, 1959), pp. 220–23. An unusual instance is Lib. *Orat.* 11.103 in which ἑλληνίζειν is evidently used transitively.

30. Athan. *Ar.* 3.16 and 4.10.

31. Eunap. *Vit. Soph. et Phil.* p. 490B.

ethnos in this earlier period.[32] The local or tribal associations of paganism are clearly indicated by the use of these terms. That the word "ethnic" should later give way to the word "Greek" as a designation for paganism suggests at one and the same time the local character of pagan cults (that is, the absence of any coherent church) and the role of Greek culture in sustaining those cults. Interestingly in this early period of the Christian church both *ethnikos* and *Hellênikos* shared a common fate in being used, in appropriate contexts, to designate gentiles in relation to Jews.[33] These two words seem to have had the general sense of "the other" (*l'autre*), indicating those who were not part of a general religious community or church.

When it came to paganism the Syriac-speaking Christians were in a less embarrassing position than their Greek-speaking neighbors. Their language had totally distinct words for pagans (*ḥanpê*) and Greeks (*yawnâyê*). It did not much matter that the Syriac word for Greek was etymologically the same as the word "Ionian." They were able to make a clear verbal distinction between Greeks (and Greek culture) and paganism (and pagan cults). The Syriac word for "pagan" has an etymological sense of "impure" or "false," and as such it had served the Syriac translators of the Greek New Testament to render both *ethnikos* and *Hellênikos* as used in the Gospels in the sense of "gentiles."[34] But this word did not serve to translate either "Greek" or "ethnic" in any extended sense beyond that.

The embarrassment of the Greek-speaking Christians over the nexus between paganism and Greek culture is nowhere more clearly expressed than in the first invective against the Emperor Julian by his Cappadocian contemporary, Gregory of Nazianzus. Julian's famous attempt to stop the Christians from teaching the pagan Greek classics was a decision of diabolical cunning, the kind of decision that only a former Christian could have made.[35] He knew that the great Christian intellectuals of his own day and before had been steeped in Greek culture and loved it. Julian, in effect, tried to force the Christians to admit that, if they repudiated *Hellênismos* in the sense of "paganism," they had at the same time to repudiate it in the sense of Greek culture. Gregory protested: "Julian has wickedly transformed the meaning of 'Greek' so as to represent a religion but not a language, and accordingly, like a thief of someone else's goods, he has stripped us of our

---

32. *Shep. Herm.* 10.1.4; Hipp. *Haer.* 7.19 (Migne *PG* 16.3302B); Clement *Paed.* 3.8 (Migne *PG* 8.613B), *Str.* 2.13 (Migne *PG* 8.993B). Lampe's lexicon of patristic Greek provides more examples.

33. Cf. Lampe's lexicon under both words.

34. *Thesaurus Syricus,* s.v. *ḥanpâ.*

35. Amm. Marc. 22.10.7, 25.4.20; *Cod. Theod.* 13.3.5. Cf. G. W. Bowersock, *Julian the Apostate* (London, 1978), pp. 83–84.

speech (*logoi*). Just as if he were to keep us from whatever arts the Greeks had devised, he thought that in this matter of language he could make it exclusively his concern because of the use of the same term (*dia tên homonumian*)."[36] Gregory then dilates on the glory of Greek as a vehicle for praising God and suggests that Julian may perhaps have aimed at removing so effective a channel to the divine ear.

Gregory clearly recognized that Julian was not trying to turn the clock back to the paganism of former times: he was trying to create something altogether new and indeed probably impossible, a pagan church.[37] Gregory also knew that the literature, rhetoric, and philosophy of the Greeks were integral to the thought and structure of Christian discourse. The real distinction that Gregory and other Christians had to make in the forms of Hellenism was that between literature and intellectual reflection, and mythology with its concomitant cults.

Another Cappadocian Christian of the same period, Basil of Caesarea, addressed this problem directly when he undertook to instruct his nephews on the value of the Greek secular classics. The words and deeds of good men deserved their close attention, but against all manifestations of polytheism their ears should be stopped like those of Odysseus in the vicinity of the Sirens. The nasty squabbles of the gods and goddesses were distinctly off limits. In Basil's words, "The adulteries of gods, their loves and public copulations, especially those of the chief god, Zeus on high, as they say, whose activities would make a reader blush—all this we shall leave to actors on the stage."[38] Basil's nephews must have been startled by these intimations of what they should not know, much as Donna Inez's son, Don Juan, in Byron's epic:

> His classic studies made a little puzzle,
>   Because of filthy loves of gods and goddesses,
> Who in the earlier ages raised a bustle,
>   But never put on pantaloons or bodices;
> His reverend tutors had at times a tussle,
>   And for their *Aeneids*, *Iliads*, and *Odysseys*,
> Were forced to make an odd sort of apology,
>   For Donna Inez dreaded the mythology.
>
> *Don Juan* I.321–28

---

36. Greg. Naz. *Orat.* 4 (*Inv. against Jul.* 1) 5.79–81.

37. W. Koch, "Comment l'empereur Julien tâcha de fonder une église païenne," four articles in *Rev. belge de phil. et d'hist.* 6 (1927) and 7 (1928).

38. Basil πρὸς τοὺς νέους 4. Cf. Yves Courtonne, *Saint Basile et l'Hellénisme* (Paris, 1934).

In the sense of literature and thought, the Christians could readily es-
pouse Greek culture, but in the sense of mythology and cult they obviously
could not. This gave an opening for the Neoplatonists of the fourth and fifth
centuries. They had no such problem and moved freely, even necessarily,
from literature and philosophy to mythology and observance. The more
extreme Neoplatonists, the so-called theurgists, or wonder-workers, who
made such a powerful impression upon the young Julian, had succeeded in
turning that branch of Neoplatonism into something very close to a religion
for pagan intellectuals.

What neither Gregory nor Basil nor Julian had perceived in their strug-
gles, because they were all fundamentally products of a common education,
was that the local cults—the ethnic cults, as the earlier Christian writers in
Greek would have put it—the cults that were still flourishing in the time of
John of Ephesus, survived in the language and mythology of the Greeks. It
was at this level that Greek culture or Hellenism really meant "paganism." It
was Greek culture that allowed the infinite multiplicity of these far-flung and
diverse cults to exist as part of a loosely defined common enterprise that we
call paganism and that the Greek-speakers of the time quite rightly called
Hellenism.

In the early third century A.D., Bardaiṣân, the sage of Edessa, said to a
disciple, "Have you read the books of the Babylonian Chaldaeans in which it
is described what influence the stars and their constellations exercised upon
the horoscopes of men, and the books of the Egyptians in which all the
different things that may befall people are described?" The disciple replied,
"I have read books on the Chaldaean doctrine, but I do not know which are
Babylonian and which are Egyptian." To which Bardaiṣân replied, "The
doctrine of both countries is the same."[39]

This dialogue, if it ever took place, was conducted in Syriac, and it is
preserved in a text in Syriac. The speakers, who thought of themselves as
Christians, are reporting on the diffusion of pagan doctrines. There was a
very good reason why they could not tell what was Babylonian from what
was Egyptian. The Chaldaean doctrine, which was to prove so influential in
the paganism of fourth-century Neoplatonists, was disseminated in Greek.

---

39. Bardaiṣân Book of the Laws of Countries p. 19 Nau, p. 40 Drijvers.

II

The Idolatry of Holiness

Neither the Jews nor the Christians had a monopoly on holiness. Piety of whatever kind can be expected to bring in its train persons and places whose apparent closeness to the divine implies the working of an other-worldly power. This is no less true of polytheism than monotheism, although the language of holiness in the great literary texts of the so-called Judaeo-Christian tradition has tended to obscure that important fact. Holiness among the pagans is richly attested across the diverse cults of the ancient world. Although the holiness that played a role in indigenous eastern cults originally had nothing to do with the Greeks, it is often best known to us through the mediation of Greek, which provided a common language for the expression of it. Fortunately in the lands of Semitic culture it is possible to disengage the native concepts of holiness both before and during the time they found their expression in Greek.

Holiness in the service of idolatry, or more precisely the idolatry represented by pagan holiness, has been rarely studied. The similarity of language in the context of a much longer tradition poses a problem for Christian exegetes, who have felt more comfortable in ascribing Semitic parallels to the safe haven of Jewish monotheism. This has meant that non-Greek and non-Jewish Semitic material generally remained out of sight. The intellectual side of later Greek paganism, as conspicuously represented by the Neoplatonic philosophers, could scarcely be ignored by Christians who themselves owed so much to Platonism, and so the role of Syrian Hellenism in late antique philosophy has fared rather better than influences of the same order at the more mundane level of local pagan cults. Yet Greek language and myth brought those disparate cults into contact with each other no less decisively than it united the philosophers of Chalcis and Apamea in Syria with the Platonists of Athens.

The pagan pantheon was full of holiness. In the various dialects of Aramaic that coexisted with Greek in the regions of Semitic polytheism, *qdyš* and related forms were used as epithets of divine beings.[1] But the Aramaic of

---

1. Cf. A. J. Festugière, *La sainteté* (Paris, 1942), p. 23, and D. Sourdel, *Les cultes du Hauran à l'époque romaine* (Paris, 1952), pp. 97–98.

Hatra or Edessa or Palmyra or Petra was by no means the same and never provided a common link for the cults of the great pagan centers, to name only a few of them. Once again it was Greek that met that need, and it did so across a broad front.

The Greek for "holy" in pagan texts, mostly epigraphical, in the Near East was usually *hagios*, a word with a good classical pedigree but somewhat confusingly (and for some, even disturbingly) the standard Greek word in imperial and Byzantine times for "saint." Hence the surprise with which some readers have happened upon current modern translations of inscriptions from pagan cult centers in the form "to Saint Uranius," the god of heaven, or "to Saint Dusares," the chief god of the Nabataeans.[2] Translating *hagios* by the word "saint" in such instances is perhaps a little mischievous on the part of an epigraphist, but it does serve to emphasize the common language of the word *hagios* in honoring pagan gods as well as the Christian one. The important point is that the pagan gods had been there longer.

Sometimes the god's name was not mentioned or was simply alluded to in the form of "the holy Arabian god," as at Gerasa, or "the holy god" at Sidon.[3] These usages in Greek mirror comparable usages in Semitic paganism.

The other Greek word for "holy," *hosios*, occurs relatively rarely in near eastern Greek; and, when it does, it tends to be in Jewish or Christian contexts.[4] It is in Asia Minor, and particularly in Phrygia, that pagan cults adopted that other term for "holiness" from the Greek repertoire.[5] There the unspecified holy one was himself a god (*ho hosios*), not unlike the unnamed holy divinity of the Near East who bore the alternative Greek epithet (*hagios*). But in Asia Minor not only the adoption of a different Greek word but the constant correlation of this word as a divine name with the deity of justice (*ho dikaios*) put beyond any doubt the indigenous character of these cults in Anatolia.[6] It is futile to see in the worship of "the holy and the just" in Phrygia (and in Lycia, too) a kind of paganism that has

---

2. Saint Uranius: *SEG* 7.2. Saint Dusares: *PEQ* 89 (1957): 13–14; *ADAJ* 24 (1980): 211, with which cf. *ADAJ* 30 (1986): 203–5.

3. C. H. Kraeling, *Gerasa* (New Haven, 1938), inscription no. 17; for Sidon, Ch. Clermont-Ganneau, *Études d'archéologie orientale* 1:100. On ἅγιος generally, E. Williger, *Hagios: Untersuchungen zur Terminologie des Heiligen in der hellenisch-hellenistischen Religion* (Giessen, 1922).

4. For example, πατέϱες ὅσιοι at Beth Shearim, *IEJ* 7 (1957): 246–47. Note, too, *Rev. biblique* 68 (1961): 401–11, inscr. no. 2 κατὰ τὴν ὁσίαν (law of the Torah).

5. For example, *Bull. épig.* 1970.527 (Lydia); *Bull. épig.* 1972.468 (Phrygia). Cf. *Bull. épig.* 1966.397 ὁσίως (Aphrodisias).

6. A. A. R. Sheppard, "Pagan Cults of Angels in Roman Asia Minor," *Talanta* 12–13 (1980–81): 77–101.

fallen under the influence of Judaism, as has recently been suggested,[7] or even of Semitic paganism—which has never been suggested and should not be.

The holiness of persons, as opposed to gods, in pagan piety was expressed by yet another epithet in Greek. Whereas both Judaism and Christianity rarely made any lexical distinction between the holiness of God and the holiness of a holy man, paganism did. The pagan holy man in late antiquity was not normally described as either *hagios* or *hosios*. His closeness to the divine was expressed by the adjectives "divine" (*theios*) or "sacred" (*hieros*).[8] Among the late philosophers, who came to have an almost priestly role, the Greek tradition drew a sharp distinction between the merely learned (*polumathês*) and the god-filled (*enthous*), to use the terminology of a Delphic oracle. Iamblichus, the Neoplatonist, was god-filled and conventionally bore the epithet "divine" (*theios*).[9] Both Plato and Pythagoras were looked upon as divine (*theioi andres*). The succession of Platonic philosophers was itself considered sacred (*hiera*), and there was talk even of a sacred—and thus exclusive—race (*hiera genea*).[10] The holy men of paganism participated in a renewal of their traditions from generation to generation. They were not isolated, blazing phenomena of superhuman godliness. They were, on the contrary, links in the great chain of Hellenism.

The living paganism of late antiquity had deep roots in traditional local cults, which shared a special characteristic that, like holiness itself, formed a parallel with Judaism and Christianity. This is a predilection for worshipping gods in groups of three. For reasons that are certainly understandable, if not excusable, historians of the early Christian church have tended to avoid the clear evidence for pagan trinities, both in their native languages and in their Greek dress. A particularly arresting illustration of this phenomenon occurs in a bilingual graffito from the Mesopotamian caravan city of Hatra.[11] First in the local Aramaic and then in Greek, three deities are

---

7. Ibid., pp. 96–98.

8. Cf. G. Fowden, "The Pagan Holy Man in Late Antique Society," *JHS* 102 (1982): 33–59. Also, R. Kirschner, "The Vocation of Holiness in Late Antiquity," *Vigiliae Christianae* 38 (1984): 105–24.

9. Many references, of which some can be found in Fowden, op. cit. (n. 8 above), p. 36 n. 18. For the persistent inability of outstanding scholars of earlier generations to understand late antique paganism, observe the appalling characterization of Iamblichus by J. Geffcken, *Der Ausgang des griechisch-römischen Heidentums* (Heidelberg, 1920), p. 104, "Der syrische Theosoph ist ein Blender ohne Glanz, ein Mensch des Scheins, dem freilich irgend eine böse Absicht fernliegt. Ganz und gar Orientale, ohne einen Rest griechisch kritischen Selbstbesinnung geht er ins Massenhafte."

10. Fowden, op. cit. (n. 8 above), p. 34 is excellent on this.

11. J. T. Milik, *Dédicaces faites par des dieux* (Paris, 1972), pp. 334–35.

invoked: one is called "our lord," the next is called "our lady," and the third is called "their son." This astonishing trio appears in Greek as Marinus, which exactly represents the Aramaic for "our lord," Marithen, which represents "our lady," and Marinus, their son. The pagan trinity of Hatra is especially remarkable for its clear definition of the relation of the three deities to one another.

Another interesting group can be seen in the Ḥawrân in southern Syria, where the coins of Bostra reveal over a long span of time altars with three idols.[12] In every case one of these idols is larger than the other two and seems to be the principal god of the trinity. A magical gem in jasper that was recorded in the nineteenth century has now provided a secure basis for identifying those three gods of the region as Dusares, the principal Nabataean deity, Ares, and Theandrios. Because of his preeminence, Dusares was undoubtedly embodied in the larger sized idol on the altars of Bostra. He was therefore flanked by Ares and Theandrios.[13] Ares is well known as an Arabian god who acquired broad currency under the familiar name of his Greek counterpart. In Palmyrene and Nabataean he was the camel-riding war god Arṣû, and it was he who gave to the city of Rabbathmoba its imperial and Byzantine name of Areopolis, the city of Ares. He is pictured on its coins; and, even for a brief period under the reign of Elagabalus, his Semitic name surfaces in the strange hybrid name Arsapolis in place of Areopolis.[14]

The third divinity of the triad was the god favored by the Neoplatonist Proclus in the fifth century A.D., Theandrios, or, as he was known later, Theandrites, meaning literally "god-man."[15] The significance of a god-man deity in an indigenous cult of Semitic paganism scarcely needs underscoring. But the failure to notice him on the part of scholars of the early Christian church is almost culpable. In the great lexicon of patristic Greek by the British scholar Lampe, the Greek word *theandritês* is glossed as a "word coined to describe Christ as a compound being."[16] Far from it: it was a word coined long before to describe the essence of a pagan god in a trinity in southern Syria.

One cannot leave the pagan trinities of the Near East without reference to a memorable triad in Palmyra. Two inscriptions in Palmyrene Aramaic from

---

12. See the examples cited in chap. 1.

13. G. W. Bowersock, "An Arabian Trinity," *Harv. Theol. Rev.* 79 (1986): 17–21.

14. E. A. Knauf, "Arsapolis: eine epigraphische Bemerkung," *Liber Annuus* 34 (1984): 353–56.

15. Cf. Bowersock, op. cit. (n. 13 above), p. 21.

16. Lampe, *Patristic Greek Lexicon*, p. 615, s.v. Θεανδρίτης.

the second century A.D. commemorate a trinity of local gods, of whom the principal one has the name of "Blessed Be His Name." Blessed Be His Name has two companions, who are known as the Two Holy Brothers or, if you prefer, the Two Brother-Saints.[17] To name a god Blessed Be His Name is a form of piety not unlike the suppression of any name at all for the so-called Arabian or holy god.

If we return to Anatolia in Asia Minor, back to the location where John of Ephesus found paganism so firmly entrenched in the sixth century, we can see another local trinity. The names of gods were rendered intelligible to the traveler Pausanias, who reported them, by their representation in Greek as Heracles, Hermes, and Apollo.[18] As Louis Robert observed, this conjunction must certainly point to translations into Greek terms of indigenous gods, and his interpretation is reinforced by the fact that the gods have a collective name, the *Spêlaitai*, "the gods of the grotto."[19] The grotto in question was a cave in the vicinity of the city of Themisonion.

Another striking feature of the idolatry of late antiquity is the invocation of angels. Like sainthood and trinities, angels, too, had a long and distinguished pedigree in paganism. Once again it was the expression of this notion in Greek that allows us to see just how widespread it was. Although the cult of pagan angels is best documented for the imperial and early Byzantine period, and especially in Greek texts, the invocation of these divine beings can be traced back as early as the third century B.C. thanks to an inscription from the territory of Tyre on the Lebanese coast. There the angel of Milkashdot is invoked as a god in the year 222 B.C.[20] This angel, like the much better known Malak Bel, or "angel of Bel," at Palmyra, is clearly an indigenous deity, destined to become more widely comprehensible with the spread of Greek as an *angelos* or "angel."

In traditional Greek literature and mythology, angels were more often messengers of the gods, only infrequently themselves gods. It was different in Semitic paganism. It was also different in the paganism of Asia Minor, where such gods as those of holiness and justice themselves qualified as angels. Greek clearly provided the medium of expression, but it did not provide the religion. In a group of interesting inscriptions from the city of Stratoniceia in Caria, a pious reluctance to utter the name of the deity can be seen in the context of angel-gods. These inscriptions show dedications to the "good

---

17. Milik, op. cit. (n. 11 above), pp. 178 and 194–96. Cf. *Syria* 12 (1931): 135–36, no. 15 (resuming *CIS* 2.4001).
18. Pausanias 10.32.3.
19. L. Robert, *Hellenica* 10.112–13, with *Berytus* 16 (1966): 36–37.
20. Milik, op. cit. (n. 11 above), p. 424 with plate 14.2.

angel" (*agathôi angelôi*), or to the "divine angel" (*theiôi angelôi*), or even in two instances to the "angelic divinity" (*theiôi angelikôi*).[21]

We have seen that a recent attempt to connect such angels of Asia Minor with Jewish communities in the area is scarcely defensible.[22] That the texts refer to local cults is made amply apparent by the references to the holy and just gods. Whether or not the angels themselves represent in Greek what were also angels in the native languages, as in the Near East, is impossible to tell. But if any influence at all is to be postulated from the Near East, it will have come naturally and easily through the *lingua franca* of eastern paganism, which was Greek. Jews and Christians had nothing to do with it.

The use of Greek language and divine nomenclature to give voice to local paganism could obviously entail gradual adjustments or even transformations in the nature of the local cults. The holy idols were nowhere so conspicuously transformed by their representation in the Hellenic medium as in the Arabian peninsula. When the Prophet Muḥammad brought down the idols of the Arabs in the seventh century A.D., he was able to point to no fewer than 360 of them in the sacred shrine of the Ka'aba.[23] The early Arab paganism of the peninsula had been far simpler. There had been only a few gods, probably a trinity but possibly only two. The chief god had his female consort, and these two, probably together with the goddess of the morning and evening star, al-'Uzzâ, provided the entire population of the early Arab pantheon.[24]

With the spread of Hellenism these gods not only acquired equivalent names in Greek, such as Athena for Allât or Aphrodite for al-'Uzzâ: they also, it will be recalled, acquired faces and bodies. For, as we have seen, the early Arabs worshipped their pagan deities in the form of nonrepresentational idols, generally stones of a vaguely pyramidal shape. Since the Greeks had a multiplicity of gods and the few Arab deities had a multiplicity of functions, it is perhaps not surprising that over the centuries more and more individual deities were separated out from the original two or three. But if the development of the pantheon and the anthropomorphic representation of its gods took place under the influence of Hellenism, the gods themselves were nonetheless all strictly Arab and local. Many of the 360 idols had no equivalent name in Greek at all, and down to the end the urge to identify a

---

21. Sheppard, op. cit. (n. 6 above): for the angelic divinity, p. 78 n. 3.

22. Sheppard's attempt, op. cit. (n. 6 above).

23. Ibn al-Athîr *Kâmil* 2.192.

24. Herod. 3.8. On al-'Uzzâ, see T. Fahd, *Le panthéon de l'Arabie centrale à la veille de l'Hégire*, Institut français d'arch. de Beyrouth, Bibliothèque arch. et hist. vol. 88 (Paris, 1968), pp. 163–82.

supreme trinity persisted. In the days of Muḥammad, according to the *Qur'ân*, there was at the center of the Arab pantheon a trinity consisting then of the familiar Allât, al-ʿUzzâ, as well as a more mysterious deity called Manât.[25]

Arab historians of Islam often had to struggle to make sense of the changes in Arab paganism down to the Muslim conquest. They developed a special vocabulary for distinguishing aniconic stones, or nonrepresentational images of gods, from idols with faces or faces and bodies.[26] They had to recognize, as Muḥammad himself did, that the increasing particularization of cults gave a greater sense of identity and belonging to the Arabs of the different parts of the peninsula. Traders, pastoralists, and farmers had an increasingly direct contact with the divinity most appropriate to their need. This is probably the explanation for the remarkable vigor of Arab self-consciousness in the centuries just before the Prophet. The many deities were worshipped together at the fairs and markets that proliferated in late antique Arabia.[27]

The remarkable role of Hellenism in strengthening and even transforming local worship without eradicating its local character is powerfully symbolized by a cult at the ancient city of Petra recorded by Epiphanius, a bishop of Salamis in Cyprus in the later fourth century A.D. In his day, he reports, the local people celebrate a virgin deity, whose name he gives in both Arabic and in its Greek equivalent, and they do so in the Arabic language (*Arabikêi dialektôi*).[28] This testimony, extraordinary enough for its revelation of Arabic hymns to a virgin goddess, goes on to say that the goddess was believed to have given birth to none other than Dusares, that ancient great god of the Nabataeans. This certainly represents something quite new in the mythology of the Near East, whether in its indigenous or its Hellenic form. Epiphanius's example from Petra comes at the conclusion of an extended discussion of a similar cult in Egyptian Alexandria.[29] He describes that cult in considerable detail, and his account, though never discussed or analyzed at length (as far as I know), is of supreme importance in understanding the late antique worship of idols. It amply merits a thorough examination, which will be attempted in what follows. The detailed and

---

25. *Qur'ân* 53.19–20.

26. Fahd, op. cit. (n. 24 above), pp. 249–51 on the terms *ṣanam* and *wathan*.

27. For the fairs, Marzûqî *Azmina* 2.161 ff.: a good discussion with further references in P. Crone, *Meccan Trade and the Rise of Islam* (Princeton, 1987), pp. 151–53, 170–80.

28. Epiphanius *Panarion* 51.22.11.

29. Ibid. 51.22.9–10. H. Rahner, *Griechische Mythen in christlicher Deutung* (Darmstadt, 1957), pp. 180–83 quotes the entire Epiphanius passage in German translation but has little of substance to say about it.

somewhat intricate argument can stand as a test case for the approach to Hellenism espoused in this book.

For most writers, paganism in Egyptian Alexandria after the death of Constantine has been something of a mystery. The destruction in 392 of the Serapeum, which the historian Ammianus Marcellinus ranked as Alexandria's most splendid temple, seemed to proclaim the doom of pagan cults.[30] It has been suggested recently by Alan Bowman that Christianity in Egypt "broke the importance of priesthoods and cult associations connected with pagan religion."[31] But the testimony of Epiphanius would suggest that this was not the case. In his work entitled *Panarion* or "Medicine Chest," designed to protect the faithful against the numerous and diverse heresies of the Christian world (paganism as such was a threat he did not address), the Cypriot bishop incidentally describes several pagan rituals in the context of his treatment of Epiphany in early January.[32]

As a parallel to the birth of Jesus Christ eight days before the Kalends of January, he invokes the Saturnalia at Rome, the Kronia (in celebration of Kronos) in Egypt, and a mysterious festival called the Kikellia in Alexandria. In particular he cites a celebration held on the night of January 5–6 in the shrine of Korê in Alexandria. At the time when he is writing, between A.D. 375 and 378,[33] the Koreion, namely the shrine dedicated to Korê, includes a very large temple. We have next an account of what happens in that shrine of Korê each year during the night in question.

We learn that the votaries stay awake all through the night in order to make music with songs and flutes to the idol of the goddess. Then, after the crowing of the cock, torchbearers descend into an underground cavern and come up with a wooden image (*xoanon*) that is naked and seated on a bier. This image is distinguished by a gold mark (*sphragis*) in the shape of a cross on its brow, and one on each of its two hands as well as one on each of its two knees.[34] The torchbearers carry the image seven times around the inmost part of the temple to the accompaniment of flutes, drums, and the singing of hymns, and finally they take it back down into the underground

---

30. Amm. Marc. 22.16.12: *His accedunt altis sufflata fastigiis templa, inter quae eminet Serapeum.*

31. A. K. Bowman, *Egypt after the Pharaohs* (Berkeley, 1986), p. 217.

32. Epiphanius *Panarion* 51.22.9–11.

33. F. Williams, trans., *The Panarion of Epiphanius of Salamis* (Leiden, 1987), 1:xiii.

34. Epiphanius *Panarion* 51.22.10: ἀναφέρουσι ξόανόν τι ξύλινον ⟨ἐν⟩ φορείῳ καθεζόμενον γυμνόν, ἔχον σφραγῖδά τινα σταυροῦ, ἐπὶ τοῦ μετώπου διάχρυσον καὶ ἐπὶ ταῖς ἑκατέραις χερσὶν ἄλλας δύο τοιαύτας σφραγῖδας καὶ ἐπ' αὐτοῖς τοῖς δυσὶ γονάτοις ἄλλας δύο . . .

cavern. In what seems to be a kind of liturgical responsion, the worshippers then ask what all this means, and the reply comes forth, "In this moment today Korê [glossed by Epiphanius as the Virgin] gave birth to Aiôn."[35]

Now Aiôn is not altogether unfamiliar to students of ancient Alexandria. The name of this rather abstract and philosophical personification appears on Alexandrian coinage of the Antonine period together with a representation of the phoenix, and both have been reasonably associated with annual rituals of death and revival.[36] A notoriously corrupt passage in Pseudo-Callisthenes has been cited from time to time in support of a Ptolemaic origin for the festival described by Epiphanius.[37] And indeed the great Otto Weinreich, early in this century, wrote a learned though curiously inconclusive study of an Eleusinian inscription honoring Aiôn in which he tried to connect the Alexandrian ritual with the Korê cult in Eleusis at the beginning of the imperial period.[38] But all of this was briskly and persuasively dismissed by Peter Fraser in his monumental work on Ptolemaic Alexandria.[39] There is simply nothing to connect the earlier intimations of Aiôn either inside or outside the city with the ceremonial observances described by Epiphanius in the latter part of the fourth century A.D.

In fact, Fraser's rejection of Epiphanius as a source for Ptolemaic or early imperial observances of an Aiôn cult can now be reinforced by additional iconographic evidence for Aiôn from the early Roman Empire. The Eleusis inscription, to which Weinreich had devoted so much attention, directly connected Aiôn, represented as a highly philosophical divinity, "who is and was and will be," with the power of Rome.[40] The dedication is not only for the endurance of the mysteries of Eleusis but also to the power of Rome (*eis kratos Rhômês*). Whatever the date of this inscription, with language like that it cannot be located very far into the Roman imperial period and would most plausibly belong near the start of it. Now the great new frieze of Zoilos discovered at Aphrodisias, commemorating the honors received by the city under Augustus through the mediation of one of the city's great citizens,

---

35. Ibid.: ταύτῃ τῇ ὥρᾳ σήμερον ἡ Κόρη (τουτέστιν ἡ παρθένος) ἐγέννησε τὸν Αἰῶνα.

36. *BMC Cat.* Alexandria, pl. 26, no. 1004; J. Vogt, *Die alexandrinischen Münzen* (Stuttgart, 1924), 1:115.

37. Pseud.-Callisthenes 1.33.2: ⟨Αἰὼν⟩ Πλουτώνιος. Cf. O. Weinreich, *Archiv für Religionswissenschaft* 19 (1916–19): 189.

38. Weinreich, op. cit., pp. 174–90. The inscription from Eleusis is *SIG*³ 1125 (*IG* II² 4705).

39. P. M. Fraser, *Ptolemaic Alexandria* (Oxford, 1972), 2:336–37.

40. Inscription cited in n. 38 above: ὁποῖος ἔστι καὶ ἦν καὶ ἔσται, ἀρχὴν μεσότητα τέλος οὐκ ἔχων, μεταβολῆς ἀμέτοχος.

contains a memorable portrait of an aged figure identified by name as Aiôn.[41] The juxtaposition of Aiôn with the ruling power as a symbol of longevity, even eternity, could not be more plain nor, under the circumstances, more appropriate. The same kind of Aiôn appeared far away in Spain, as Andreas Alföldi observed about ten years ago, in the great cosmological mosaic at Merida.[42] The motifs in that mosaic seem to be Hellenistic in inspiration, but the appearance of Aeternitas, who would appear to be the Latin equivalent of Aiôn, suggests once again the use of this philosophical divinity to guarantee the permanence of imperial rule.

This Aiôn of the early empire could hardly be further removed from the Aiôn of the Epiphanius passage. The Eleusis text, the Aphrodisias frieze, and the Merida mosaic suggest that there was a self-consciously ideological use of Aiôn in the early empire that was directly connected with the establishment of Roman imperial power. This would imply therefore that there was no anterior cult of Aiôn at Alexandria in the Ptolemaic period, as Fraser had already insisted, and furthermore that the Aiôn of the early empire had nothing to do with the Aiôn of the fourth century A.D. The Antonine coins at Alexandria in the intervening period are another matter, as will emerge.

It has rarely been noticed that, after his invocation of the Alexandrian parallel to Epiphany, Epiphanius goes on to provide two other parallels, though in somewhat less detail. One is a ceremony at Petra in Transjordan, the other at Elusa in the Negev Desert. The Elusa parallel is less illuminating, since all we are told is that the celebration goes on during the same night as the other two, but we hear nothing more about it. For Petra, however, the matter is different. The nocturnal rite of January 5–6 takes place there in their pagan shrine (*eidôleion*). As we have seen already, the natives hymn the Virgin, that is Korê, in Arabic, and they name her in their language Khaamou or Khaabou (the exact form of the name is immaterial here). Just as at Alexandria, a virgin birth is proclaimed, but the offspring at Petra is, instead of Aiôn, none other than Dusares, the great deity of the Nabataeans. He is obviously exhibited as a baby, despite a traditional Semitic antipathy to depictions of their gods as anything less than full-grown.[43]

---

41. A. Alföldi, with contributions by E. Alföldi-Rosenbaum, K. T. Erim, and J. Reynolds, *Madrider Beiträge* 6 (1979). See also Marie-Henriette Quet, *La mosaïque cosmologique de Mérida* (1981), pp. 153–84.

42. Ibid.

43. Epiphanius *Panarion* 51.22.11: τὸν ἐξ αὐτῆς γεγεννημένον Δουσάρην τουτέστιν μονογενῆ τοῦ δεσπότου. The alleged translation is still unexplained. For a plausible interpretation of the mother's Arabic name, see Crone, op. cit. (n. 27 above), p. 192. On baby gods see Lucian, *De Dea Syria* 35. Cf. J. Wellhausen, *Reste arabischen Heidentums*, 2d ed. (Berlin and Leipzig, 1927), p. 50 n. 1: "Von einem *divine child* Dusares redet übrigens Epiphanius über-

Epiphanius's example from Petra accordingly makes explicit what is left obscure in the case of Alexandria, and that is that Korê and her offspring are deemed to represent indigenous deities in this rite. In the case of Petra, the child brought forth is the supreme deity of the region. We are perhaps authorized to infer therefore that the same is true of the newborn child in the ritual at Alexandria. On the mosaics at New Paphos on Cyprus Aiôn clearly appears as the ranking god in a beauty contest in which Cassiopeia emerges victorious. We must at least assume that the Alexandrian Aiôn represents a major Egyptian deity, who could lay some claim to being the supreme god.

Fortunately, two important passages in the Suda Lexicon, one of which is explicitly ascribed to Damascius in his *Life of Isidore*, not only confirm the importance of Aiôn in late antique Alexandria, as suggested by Epiphanius, but clearly identify the Egyptian deity that he embodies. A psychic personality by the name of Heraiscus, who had an exceptional knowledge of Egyptian wisdom, recognized, we are told, that the statue of Aiôn, about which one did not speak (*to arrêton agalma tou Aiônos*), was possessed by the god whom the Alexandrians honored, namely Osiris and Adonis, one and the same representation of the god of death and renewal.[44] The identification of Aiôn with Osiris is likewise implied in the explicit quotation from Damascius in the Suda, where reference is made to a certain priest who presided over the rites of Osiris, *ou monon de, alla kai tôn tou Aiônos humnoumenou theou*, "not only his rites but those of the hymned god Aiôn."[45] The ineffable character of Aiôn, hinted at in the phrase *to arrêton agalma*, is borne out by Damascius, who says that, although he was able to say what the nature of Aiôn was, he would not do so.[46]

Accordingly, we have the Hellenic philosophical deity Aiôn, tenanted by Osiris, or, in another Hellenic form, Adonis, as the deity to whom the virgin Korê gave birth annually on the morning of January 6. Now, apart from the use of a Hellenic mystery cult to embody and perpetuate the local traditions, we have the remarkable character of the image of Aiôn that is brought forth from the underground cavern and taken seven times around the holy of

---

haupt nicht [*sic*]. Kein Semit hat sich je seinen Gott als ein Kind vorgestellt." This is not to be altogether believed.

44. Suda, s.v. Ἡραῖσκος: οὕτω διέγνω τὸ ἄρρητον ἄγαλμα τοῦ Αἰῶνος ὑπὸ τοῦ θεοῦ κατεχόμενον, ὃν Ἀλεξανδρεῖς ἐτίμησαν, Ὄσιριν ὄντα καὶ Ἄδωνιν. The discussion of Messalla Rufus, cos. 53 B.C., as a source on Aiôn in R. Reitzenstein, *Poimandres* (Leipzig, 1904), makes no reference to Alexandria.

45. Suda, s.v. Ἐπιφάνιος.

46. Ibid.: ὃν ἔχων εἰπεῖν ὅστις ἐστίν, ὅμως οὐ γράφω κατά γε τὴν παροῦσαν ταύτην ὁρμήν. For a recent discussion of Alexandrian Aiôn, see R. Merkelbach, *Isisfeste in griechisch-römischer Zeit* (Meisenheim, 1963), pp. 47–50. On p. 48 Korê is identified with Isis.

holies. Epiphanius says that the five marks in the shape of a cross were impressed (*tetupômenas*) in gold, and it would seem that this must mean some kind of gold inlay representing a physical *stigma*. No one has ever been able to suggest what this peculiar pattern of markings on the image might mean. One thing is certain: a bishop such as Epiphanius cannot have intended to describe the Egyptian *ankh* when he carefully used the word *stauros*. Epiphanius's selection of the Alexandrian ritual as a pagan parallel for a Christian observance, together with the fact that in it a virgin gives birth, ought to point to the answer.

Apart from a Cretan legend of the birth of Zagreus, nothing in the entire Greek mythological tradition suggests that Korê, or as she is otherwise known, Persephone, the bride of Hades, ever gave birth at all. She was and remained a virgin; and, although there are some hints of virgin birth in ancient sources, nowhere as far as I know was this ever associated with Korê in the Near East until late antiquity.[47] Similarly, in the ritual at Petra nowhere had the god Dusares ever before been commemorated as the product of a virgin birth. In these two cases at least, one is dealing with the invention or fabrication of a new tradition involving indigenous deities represented in Hellenic form. Epiphanius is suggesting, by the very parallels that he adduces, that this has something to do with the Christian tradition of Jesus Christ.

It is very important to remember here that Christianity had a powerful influence on the paganism that prospered in the late antique world, to a degree, I suggest, no less important than the influence—much more frequently remarked—of paganism on Christianity. You will recall that Julian the Apostate is a prime exhibit. Born and brought up as a Christian, he used what he learned as a child to try to make paganism a more successful rival to Christianity. He imported the idea of charity and alms-giving into the pagan cults that he attempted to revive. Pagan iconography, likewise, shows as much the influence of Christian iconography (particularly in respect to the Virgin and Child) as Christian shows the influence of pagan.[48] The mark of the cross on the forehead, hands, and knees of the *xoanon* of Aiôn can nat-

---

47. For Zagreus, Callim. *Aetia* frag. 43, l. 117 Pfeiffer; Diod. Sic. 5.75.4. Cf. Eur. *Cret.* frag. 472, l. 11 Nauck². In the fifth century A.D. Nonnos *Dionys.* 5.565–71, 6.155–68 gives the first generalized account of Korê as a virgin mother.

48. Cf. G. W. Bowersock, *Julian the Apostate* (London and Harvard, 1978), p. 87; also id., "From Emperor to Bishop: the Self-Conscious Transformation of Political Power in the Fourth Century A.D.," *Class. Phil.* 81 (1986): 299. See also the striking example of Hermes holding the infant Dionysus in pl. 2.

urally be explained as the importation of Christian stigmata on the pseudo-Christ child, whether Aiôn or Osiris is seen to be in the Alexandrian ritual.

The cross on the forehead, either symbolically bestowed through a gesture or physically represented by being painted or tattooed, is well documented in early ecclesiastical sources. In addition the stigmata elsewhere on the body were known to the Christian tradition from Paul's celebrated but imprecise remark in the Epistle to the Galatians that he possessed on his own body the marks of Jesus (*ta stigmata tou Iêsou*).[49] In later tradition hands and feet were the customary locations of these marks, but anywhere that Jesus suffered was possible (shoulders and back are both attested). So there is nothing intrinsically improbable about hands and knees. Aiôn, presented as the pagan Jesus, bears these marks in just the same way as the pagan Mary, Persephone or Korê, experiences a virgin birth. The pagan god is, of course, born again each year, and accordingly unlike Jesus he arrives in the world equipped with stigmata already as a baby.

Being the embodiment of Osiris, Aiôn emerged as the supreme pagan deity of late antique Egypt.[50] Furthermore, those Antonine coins depicting the phoenix with the legend of Aiôn can now be interpreted as an early stage in Alexandria's equation of Aiôn with Osiris, clearly associated with the phoenix as a creature of death and renewal.[51] This Aiôn is thus demonstrably far removed from the Aiôn of Eleusis or of Aphrodisias.

Unfortunately we lack for Korê herself an explicit ancient indication of the local deity she represented, even though for Petra Epiphanius obligingly provides this information. Isis seems a likely candidate, especially since a tradition proclaiming her a virgin who gave birth without male cooperation seems to have acquired currency in late antiquity.[52] But further speculation would be idle here. What we have already deduced about Aiôn and Osiris, virgin birth, and the marks of a cross serves well enough.

Epiphanius on the Koreion at Alexandria affords a unique glimpse into the process by which idolatry in Egypt adapted to the newly Christianized empire of Byzantium. Above all, he shows the exceptional flexibility and power of Greek mythology in assuring the survival of indigenous cults at Alexandria as at Petra. Hellenism (*Hellênismos*) gave such local cults a new tenacity in the Christian empire. Its language was the universal language of

---

49. Gal. 6.17. Cf. C. P. Jones, *JRS* 77 (1987): 150.

50. Cf. L. Kákosy, *Oriens Antiquus* 3 (1964): 15–25.

51. Ibid., p. 22.

52. *Zeitschrift für ägyptische Sprache und Altertumskunde* 33 (1917): 94–97, cited by J. G. Griffiths, *Plutarch's De Iside et Osiride* (Oxford, 1970), p. 284.

paganism. Its myths and idols were infinitely serviceable. Because Byzantine Christianity was also Greek, the holy ones and the holy places of paganism, together with the idolatry they represented, could be subtly transformed to accommodate the tastes and images that Christians had popularized. Once again we have another demonstration of why the word "Hellenism" came to mean "paganism."

III

The Syrian Tradition

Alexander the Great opened the Near East to Greek language and culture. Hellenism had not been unknown before he passed that way, but after him its diffusion throughout the cities and countryside was irreversible. Among the successors of Alexander, the Seleucid monarchs assumed control of the vast but culturally coherent region of greater Syria, extending from the Phoenician coast in the west all the way to northern Mesopotamia. Although the archaeological traces of Hellenistic Syria are frustratingly few,[1] the powerful impact of Greek culture can be seen everywhere a few centuries later in the early Roman imperial province of Syria. The caravan city of Palmyra was completely bilingual. Its indigenous deities were worshipped under both Greek and native names in monumental structures that drew their inspiration from Hellenic temples. The same was true at Damascus, Emesa, and Bostra, to name only a few of the more important cities of central Syria. In the more distant reaches of Osrhoene in Mesopotamia the Greek language made slower progress than the Greek gods, largely because Syriac was proving to be a widely understood means of communication. Just as Palmyrene and Nabataean were dying out in the third century A.D., Syriac was developing in the north into a flexible and eloquent instrument of sophisticated expression.

But in the villages and rural areas of central and southern Syria, Greek can once again be seen as the language of local piety, uniting worshippers from shrines and holy places that lay far apart. It is too little appreciated that in general Greek inscriptions are far more common in the countryside of late antique Syria than Syriac ones, as Enno Littmann pointed out over half a century ago.[2] A few examples will readily illustrate the mediating role of Greek outside the cities—a role that needs to be stressed because Hellenism is conventionally associated with urbanism in the Near East. The mistake of

---

1. Cf. F. Millar, "The Problem of Hellenistic Syria," in *Hellenism in the East*, ed. A. Kuhrt and S. Sherwin-White (London, 1987), pp. 110–33.

2. E. Littmann, *Princeton Arch. Exp. Syria* 4.B, p. 24. See also H. Kennedy and J. H. W. G. Liebeschuetz, "Antioch and the Villages of Northern Syria in the Fifth and Sixth Centuries A.D.: Trends and Problems," *Nottingham Medieval Studies* 32 (1988): 65–90.

connecting Greek with the cities arises from the unfortunate habit of concentrating exclusively on Christian culture, in which Hellenophone bishops can be contrasted with Syriac-speaking monks.

Let us look at the Ḥawrân of southern Syria. At the village of Sammet al-Baradan, a tidily composed inscription, cut into a block of local basalt, records that it was part of a dedication set up by a man and his son. The Greek is rudimentary but serves the purpose: "Ausos, Obaidos his son, both of them made this gift to Ilaalges and to his angel (*angelôi*), Idarouma."[3] Both names are Greek forms of Semitic names and designate without any doubt indigenous residents of the region. They have made their dedication to a Semitic god who appears in the curious Greek form of Ilaalges, representing the Semitic (or more precisely the Arabic) elements *Allah al-ji*, "the god of al-ji." (The *jîm* was pronounced hard, as it still is in Egypt today.) Al-ji is well known as a sacred locality adjacent to Petra in Nabataea to the south. This is none other than the god of that remote locality being worshipped far away to the north. Furthermore, the text makes reference to this god's angel—another and very remarkable pagan angel—, Idarouma. His name is once again a Greek representation of Semitic (or Arabic) elements: *ida* means "the hand" and *rouma* represents the participle "raised." This is an angel that is a raised hand—not an angel *with* a raised hand but an angel that is the hand itself. Coins of southern Syria depict precisely the raised hand with the palm toward the viewer as a kind of secondary deity.[4] The connection between the divine hand and the god of al-ji at Petra is therefore established by a Greek text from an epoch when the local Semitic languages were no longer much written, even though they were spoken.

Another stunning illustration of the role of Hellenism in rural Syria can be found in a group of funerary inscriptions recently published from Yussef Pasha along the Euphrates.[5] The site is a burial area or *hypogeum* containing three burial chambers (*loculi*) cut into the rock. Inscriptions in Greek name those who were laid to rest there. The names, taken together, call up poignantly the mixed culture of Syria, both indigenous and Graeco-Roman. A Flavius Longinus brings together the family name of the imperial dynasty founded by Vespasian and a Latin *nomen* that was widely used in the Greek East. It was particularly associated with one of the intimates of Queen Zenobia at Palmyra. But other names in the same place are totally Semitic in Greek form. These include Ouabaios, of which the first element evokes

---

3. J. T. Milik, *Dédicaces faites par des dieux* (Paris, 1972), p. 428: Αὖσος ᾽Οβαιδος υἱὸς οἱ δύο δῶρον ἐπόησαν ᾽Ιλααλγη καὶ τῷ ἀνγέλῳ αὐτοῦ ᾽Ιδαρουμα.

4. Ibid., pl. 13.

5. G. W. Clarke, "Funerary Inscriptions near Joussef Pasha, North Syria," *Abr-Nahrain* 26 (1988): 19–29.

the Semitic *whb*, meaning "gift," as in the well-known Syrian name
Vaballathus. The name Baroiaros displays in Greek the Aramaic word for
"son" (*bar*), presumably to render a patronymic. The rest of the name is a
rendition of the Semitic elements *w'r*, which can be seen in other texts in the
form *ouaros*—to be carefully distinguished from the Roman name Varus.
These humble texts show the importance of Greek in a part of Syria where
again the local written language was virtually extinct. Where it was not,
notably in Edessa, the Hellenic inheritance comes through in other, but no
less significant ways.

In 1956 a mosaic was discovered at Turkish Urfa, site of the ancient
Edessa, containing one of the very rare examples of a Greek mythological
scene with an accompanying text in a local language, in this case Syriac.[6]
The mosaic shows Orpheus with his lyre and an appreciative audience of
friendly animals, including several birds, a lion, and a deer, as well as two
winged, but otherwise evidently human figures who call the attention of the
onlooker to the inscription. These winged figures are best interpreted as
angels of Orpheus in a city that was already a major center of eastern
Christianity. Orpheus himself is identified, for the benefit of the viewer, in
clear Syriac letters alongside his head. The whole piece is dated to A.D.
227/28.

The mosaic of Orpheus at Edessa therefore belongs to the same general
period as the work of the earliest Syriac Christian writer, Bardaiṣân. Although Bardaiṣân's views came under serious attack from Christians in subsequent centuries, particularly from Ephraem in the fourth, it is the very
irregularity of his Christian doctrines that makes him interesting. For, like
the pagan designer of the Orpheus mosaic, he is, as a Christian, conspicuously under the influence of Greek attitudes and forms. These are best
seen in the work entitled "The Book of the Laws of Countries," in which he
is the principal interlocutor. This work shows an interest in astrology that
subsequently proved embarrassing for Christians. But it consorted admirably with the astrological enthusiasms of the Arab bedouin tribes and of the
sedentary citizens of the nearby city of Carrhae, which contained a celebrated shrine of the moon. Bardaiṣân claims in the treatise to have read both
the Chaldaean and the Egyptian writings on horoscopes and the stars, and it
is evident that he must have done this in the language in which these works
were then disseminated, namely Greek.[7] In fact, the Chaldaean oracles,
which were to have such a great impact on Neoplatonists of the fourth

---

6. J. B. Segal, *Edessa: The Blessed City* (Oxford, 1970), pl. 44. For the text on the mosaic,
H. J. W. Drijvers, *Old-Syriac (Edessean) Inscriptions* (Leiden, 1972), pp. 40–41, no. 50.

7. See the end of chap. 1.

century (including the Emperor Julian), had only recently surfaced—or been created—in Greek form in the preceding century and, significantly, in Syria.[8]

It is not only Bardaiṣân's understanding of the Greek transmission of Chaldaean and Egyptian astrology that shows his debt to Syrian Hellenism. It is the very form of the work in which he appears. "The Book of the Laws of Countries" is a dialogue that is structured quite clearly on a Platonic model, according to which Bardaiṣân plays the role of Socrates. The opening of the dialogue itself is startlingly reminiscent of the opening of Plato's "Republic." Plato's great work begins in a celebratedly offhand manner: "I went down yesterday to the Piraeus with Glaucon, the son of Ariston, to pray to the goddess and at the same time wanting to see in what way they would celebrate the festival there now for the first time."[9] Compare with this the opening of "The Book of the Laws of Countries": "A few days ago we went to visit our brother, Shemashgram, when Bardaiṣân came and found us there. After he had embraced him and seen he was well, he asked us, 'What were you talking about?'"[10] The Platonic model of the form of "The Book of the Laws of Countries" has been noted occasionally, but its implications for Greek culture in Edessa have only rarely been appreciated.

The hint of Platonism provided by Bardaiṣân provides some help in understanding why Syria became such a notorious breeding ground of late antique Neoplatonism in subsequent centuries. The most influential of the Neoplatonists who advocated miraculous manipulation of the gods, according to the doctrines known as theurgy, was Iamblichus in the early fourth century, the single most important Neoplatonist between the death of Plotinus and the school of Proclus. Iamblichus was steeped in the Chaldaean oracles and the Hermetic writings of Egypt, as well as the writings of Plato (particularly the most abstruse and obscure). He was based in Syrian Apamea in the fourth century, where his influence as a teacher was enormous. There is a direct line through his pupils to the conversion of Julian from Christianity to paganism.[11]

---

8. H. Lewy, *Chaldaean Oracles and Theurgy: Mysticism, Magic, and Platonism in the Later Roman Empire*, ed. M. Tardieu (Paris, 1978).

9. Plato *Resp.* 327a.

10. Bardaiṣân *Book of the Laws of Countries* p. 1 Nau, p. 4 Drijvers. Note that Sebastian Brock, "From Antagonism to Assimilation: Syriac Attitudes to Greek Learning," in *Syriac Perspectives on Late Antiquity*, Variorum Reprints (London, 1984), V.19, recognizes Bardaiṣân's use of "the Greek dialogue form." Brock's article is reprinted from *East of Byzantium*, Dumbarton Oaks Symposium, ed. N. Garsoian, T. Matthews, and R. Thomson (Washington, D.C., 1982), pp. 12–34.

11. For an excellent, brief account of Iamblichus, see G. Fowden, *The Egyptian Hermes* (Cambridge, 1986), pp. 131–41.

Apamea itself, now splendidly excavated, has emerged as a great Greek city that was obviously hospitable to Iamblichus. Its mosaics include a spectacular and innovative representation of the myth of Cassiopeia and, most remarkably, a scene of the Seven Sages at table in which Socrates is the central figure.[12] The parallelism with Jesus and his Disciples is so striking that we may well have here another example of a pagan response to Christian motifs.[13] In late antiquity the Sages were also well known to the Christians as prophets of their faith (by selective quotation, to be sure), and so the mosaic could conceivably even have a Christian interpretation.[14] But in dating it to the reign of Julian, the excavator has argued that in the figure of Socrates himself we are meant to understand the pagan emperor.[15] Although this hypothesis obviously lies beyond proof, it is attractive. The representation of Socrates is not in doubt, since his name is set in the mosaic above his head. And the very presence of Socrates in this great center of late antique Platonism is eloquent enough.

The link that binds together the astrological speculations of Bardaiṣân and the theurgy of Iamblichus was understandably something that unnerved the Syriac-speaking Christians of the fourth century. These contemporaries of Iamblichus and his pupils were most forcefully represented by Ephraem of Edessa. That marvelous poet, whose control of the Syriac language and whose subtle use of metaphor has justly led to comparisons with Pindar and Dante, notoriously did not trust the Greeks or their culture.[16] What is more important still is that he had no need of Greek. His own language was a more than adequate instrument for expounding his Christian theology. In this respect, accordingly, he was far removed from the tribulations that afflicted his contemporaries, Gregory of Nazianzus and Basil of Caesarea. Both Gregory and Basil wrote brilliantly in the Greek that paganism had bequeathed to them, but after Julian they became acutely aware of the problem of combining pagan rhetoric with Christian devotion. This is, of course, the fundamental problem of Hellenism as Greek culture and as paganism. Perhaps the most important fact about the Syriac-speaking Chris-

---

12. J.-Ch. Balty, *Guide d'Apamée* (Brussels, 1981), p. 187 (Socrates and sages), p. 212 (Nereids with Cassiopeia).

13. J. and J.-Ch. Balty, "Julien et Apamée: Aspects de la restauration de l'hellénisme et de la politique antichrétienne de l'empereur," *Dialogues d'histoire ancienne* 1 (1974): 267–304.

14. Sebastian Brock, "Some Syriac Excerpts from Greek Collections of Pagan Prophecies," *Vigiliae Christianae* 38 (1984): 77–90.

15. Balty and Balty, op. cit. (n. 13 above).

16. For a general appreciation and reassessment, see Sidney H. Griffith, "Ephraem, the Deacon of Edessa, and the Church of the Empire," in *Diakonia: Studies in Honor of Robert T. Meyer* (Washington, D.C., 1986), pp. 22–52.

tians was that the problem seemed at first not to exist for them at all. Their Christian theology did not have to be expressed in Greek.

Ephraem, now recognized actually to have known more Greek than once was thought, nonetheless felt free to denounce both the Greeks and their culture. In his *Hymns on the Faith* he wrote the memorable line, "Blessed is the one who has never tasted the poison of the wisdom of the Greeks."[17] Here, as Sebastian Brock has observed, Ephraem is using the exact Syriac equivalent (*hekmta d-yawnâyê*) of Athanasius's phrase *hê sophia tôn Hellê-nôn* ("the wisdom of the Greeks"), which should properly be rendered "pagan wisdom."[18] On the other hand, there is little reason to believe that Ephraem could have made (or would have made) the distinction between Greeks as cultural carriers and Greeks as pagans. After all, in another place he wrote, "The accursed dialectic is vermin from the Greeks."[19] If Ephraem's principal targets were paganism and the logic-chopping ways of philosophers, as they undoubtedly were, he cannot conceal an evident satisfaction that he and his Syrian coreligionists have no need to rub shoulders with the pagans by communicating in the same language as they do. In Brock's words, "Greek mythology was never part of the cultural baggage of the past for the Syriac church as it was for the Greek."[20]

But the isolation of the Syriac church was bound not to last. The New Testament itself was in Greek, and that could not be undone. The early Syriac translation of the New Testament proved increasingly unsatisfactory, and the work had to be done again. Much of the most important writing on Christianity, both homiletic and hagiographical, was in Greek, and the Syriac communities could not afford to be ignorant of it.[21] Homiletic forms were themselves influenced by Greek principles of rhetoric, and these gradually took control of homilies in Syriac. A century after Ephraem, one of the leaders of the Syriac church, Philoxenos of Mabbûg, faulted the poetic diction of Ephraem as imprecise. He even went so far as to declare, "Our Syriac tongue is not accustomed to use the precise terms that are in currency with the Greeks."[22] This meant that an increasing amount of translation from Greek into Syriac was called for, and that in turn provided new strength for paganism as well as for Christianity.

---

17. Ephraem *De fide*, CSCO 154:7.
18. Brock, op. cit. (n. 10 above), p. 19.
19. Ephraem *De fide*, CSCO 154:268.
20. Brock, op. cit. (n. 10 above), p. 19.
21. See all of Brock's important papers, op. cit. (n. 10 above).
22. Philoxenos, CSCO 231:51.

In short, the Syriac speakers brought into their Christian church the very problem that Ephraem believed he did not have. It was bound to happen. Like Coptic in Egypt, which at first seemed to provide a truly indigenous national form of Christianity, Syriac began as the language of a people uncontaminated by Hellenism but turned out, in the end, to be more contaminated than anyone had realized. And, in fact, it was in dire need of further contamination in order to survive.

In the fifth and sixth centuries the Syriac church became increasingly Hellenized, both through translations that were made and through the introduction of Greek words into the Syriac lexicon. Even the Greek word for "poetry" was taken over into Syriac as *po'itûtha*, and as such it was often a synonym for Greek mythology, hence error.[23] But the Syriac church had to deal with it nonetheless. Some of its more sophisticated writers could even find virtue in it. Isaac of Antioch, writing in the late fifth century, began one of his poems with a quotation from a pagan Greek writer: "I heard a poet of the world magnifying virginity, and I rejoice that even with pagans the choice of virginity is something weighty."[24]

In Syria, as elsewhere, the pagans themselves watched in a spirit of emulation the developments of Syriac Christian literature. Its great contribution to hagiography, as shown in the lives of Ephraem or of Rabbûla, in Zacharias's life of Severus, or in the *Saints' Lives* by John of Ephesus, began to find a mirror image in the Syrian lives of pagan holy men. Porphyry's *Life of Plotinus* was the forerunner, but equally distinguished and clearly in the style of Christian hagiography was Marinus's *Life of Proclus* and Damascius's *Life of Isidore*—two of the greatest holy men of late antique Neoplatonism.[25] It will be recalled that Marinus came from Neapolis in Palestine, very close to the culture of southern Syria, and that Damascius came from the city for which he was named, Damascus. The pagan response to the Syriac saints' lives is an important reflection, sometimes overlooked or underestimated, of late antique Hellenism in Syria.

Many centers of Greek culture included substantial pagan communities. At a famous enquiry into pagan activity held at Constantinople in the sixth century, leading figures were brought together from Athens, Syrian Antioch,

---

23. Brock, op. cit. (n. 10 above), p. 28.
24. *Homiliae S. Isaaci Syri Antiocheni*, ed. Bedjan, p. 675.
25. Cf. R. Masullo, introduction to her edition of Marinus, *Vita di Proclo* (Naples, 1985), p. 23: "La vita d'ascesi, la rinuncia alla ricchezze, le forme di penitenza a cui viene sottoposto il corpo ricordano molto da vicino il tipo di vita di un monaco cristiano, il cui unico scopo è la raggiungimento della perfezione spirituale."

and Syrian Heliopolis (Baʿalbek).[26] The paganism of Heliopolis is well documented in the sources and seems comparable in intensity to that of Carrhae (Ḥarrân) where the cult of the planets, especially the moon, seems to have gone on unabated.[27] As late as the end of the sixth century or the beginning of the seventh, a work was addressed to the pagans of Ḥarrân incorporating Syriac translations of assorted prophecies of pagan philosophers.[28] These had been obviously circulating widely in Greek as sacred texts for the pagans (who had traditionally not had sacred texts). The Christians now tried to draw out of those texts suitable quotations to persuade the pagans that their own philosophers and sages had anticipated the coming of Christ. This remarkable selection of prophetic excerpts was taken from Orpheus, Hermes Trismegistos, Plato, Sophocles, Pythagoras, Porphyry, and the Sibylline Oracles. It was reasonably assumed that the anthology would carry some weight with the pagans of Ḥarrân, who were known to display a quotation from Plato in Syriac on one of their temples. As late as the tenth century, the Arab historian Masʿûdî had seen this text and conversed with the philosophers who frequented the temple.[29]

In nearby Edessa sacrifices were made at the temple of Zeus as late as the end of the sixth century.[30] The survival of such rites in the most important center of the Syriac church tells its own story. So late a date for the public celebration of Greek pagan cults is but one of many illustrations of the failure of imperial legislation against paganism to have much effect. Two hundred years earlier in Osrhoene, and probably at Edessa itself, Christians had tried to close down a pagan temple, but Theodosius had responded by forbidding divinatory sacrifices while leaving the temple open.[31] Despite fifth-century legislation against pagan cults, Rabbûla, the bishop of Edessa, was able to find four sanctuaries to close down.[32] By the end of the fifth century pagan festivals were still being celebrated with enthusiasm by a substantial part of the population of the city. These festivals included dancing, the telling of pagan stories, all-night vigils, and lascivious conduct.[33]

---

26. Michael Syr. 2.271.

27. John of Eph. *Hist. Eccles.* 3.3.27, CSCO 106, Scrip. Syri 55:154 bottom (Syriac) on Heliopolis. For Ḥarrân, see Sebastian Brock, "A Syriac Collection of Prophecies of the Pagan Philosophers," *Orientalia Lovaniensia Periodica* 14 (1983): 203–46.

28. Brock, op. cit. (n. 27 above).

29. The text of Masʿûdî is quoted and discussed by M. Tardieu in his article, "Ṣâbiens coraniques et «ṣâbiens» de Ḥarrân," *Journal asiatique* 274 (1986): 1–44, especially at pp. 13–14. The quotation from the Platonic corpus comes from I *Alc.* 133c.

30. Evagrius *Hist. Eccles.* 5.18; John of Ephesus, op. cit. (n. 27 above) 3.3.28, p. 155 (Syriac).

31. Segal, op. cit. (n. 6 above), p. 92.

32. Ibid., p. 106.

33. Note recently W. Cramer, "Irrtum und Lüge: Zum Urteil des Jakob von Sarug über

The vigor of Syrian paganism at the beginning of the sixth century is nowhere better attested than in two Syriac homilies of Jacob of Serûg, known as "the flute of the Holy Spirit and harp of the believing church." This prolific writer, author of 760 metrical homilies, was a *periodeutes*—a kind of country priest—in the region southwest of Edessa for many years until he became Bishop of Batnai at an advanced age in A.D. 519. His homily on the fall of the idols and several others on Greek theatrical entertainments present a colorful picture of pagan life in late antique Syria.[34] Although Jacob makes use of many traditional arguments against the unbelievers, much of what he says suggests firsthand knowledge.

He provides a register of pagan cults in Syria: Apollo in Antioch, Nabu and Bel in Edessa, Sîn and Ba'alshamîn in Harrân. He records hilltop shrines to Ares and Hermes, a valley dedicated to Heracles.[35] The list of gods and goddesses includes, as in these representative samples, both native and Greek names, but this must not be understood, as it sometimes has been, to show two distinct forms of pagan piety. Jacob himself viewed all the cults as bound up with Greek culture, just as the Harrânians did in giving pride of place to Plato in Syriac among the temples of their native deities. In his homily on the fall of the idols Jacob contrasts the chosen of God (the Christian god) with the pagan idols in gold and silver. He says that Christ seems but a pygmy among the mighty companions of Heracles, and an ignorant rustic among the Greek philosophers. Yet our Lord confounds them.[36] The reference to Greek philosophers here is very telling.

In his homilies on public entertainments Jacob of Serûg describes the popularity of pantomimes in the theaters of Syrian cities. His account depicts with indignation the dancing that was characteristic of these spectacles and the Greek mythological stories they enacted—Ares and Aphrodite, Leda and the swan, Danaë and the shower of gold, and other lubricious tales of gods and goddesses. The enthusiasm of the audiences moves Jacob to declare, "Satan wishes to set up paganism by means of the play."[37]

Reste paganer Religion und Kultur," *Jahrbuch für Antike und Christentum* 23 (1980): 96–107. For more general studies of paganism in late antique Syria, see H. Drijvers, "The Persistence of Pagan Cults and Practices in Christian Syria," in *East of Byzantium* (n. 10 above), pp. 35–43, reprinted in H. Drijvers, *East of Antioch*, Variorum (London, 1984), item XVI. See also W. Kaegi, "The Fifth Century Twilight of Byzantine Paganism," *Classica et Medievalia* 27 (1966): 243–75.

34. Abbé Martin, "Discours de Jacques de Saroug sur la chute des idoles," ZDMG 29 (1875): 107–47; C. Moss, "Jacob of Serugh's Homilies on the Spectacles of the Theatre," *Le Muséon* 48 (1935): 87–112.

35. Martin, op. cit. (n. 34 above), pp. 110–12.

36. Ibid., pp. 117–18.

37. Moss, op. cit. (n. 34 above), p. 98 (end of fragment of Homily 3).

Jacob acknowledges that Christians among the viewers would naturally defend themselves against any charges of impropriety. In an important (though often neglected) passage he produces their arguments: "It is a game, not paganism. What do you lose if I laugh? The dancing of that place cheers me up, and while I confess God I also take pleasure in the play . . . I am baptized just as you are." To all this Jacob sourly replies, "Who can wallow in mud without being dirty?" The dynamism of late antique pantomimes was bound up, in Jacob's mind, with the Greeks, because of the myths they depict. Hence, despite the Roman origins of pantomime, he can refer to "the folly which the Greeks invented" and to "the dancing of the Greeks."[38] By Greeks he certainly means Greeks rather than pagans, for which he uses the normal Syriac word *ḥanpê* and its related forms. Jacob tells us in effect that Hellenism is what makes paganism flourish.

The sacrifices at the temple of Zeus in Edessa at the end of the sixth century are known to us from the denouement of an elaborate assault on pagan practices throughout Syria at that time.[39] It serves to illustrate how widespread they were. The trouble began either at the end of the reign of Justin II or a decade or so later under Tiberius II, when the citizens of Heliopolis (Baʿalbek), largely worshippers of the great Heliopolitan triad of deities, launched a persecution of the Christians. In his *Ecclesiastical History* John of Ephesus says that the people of Heliopolis openly worshipped Satan and enjoyed widespread wealth and prosperity there, whereas the Christians, who were both few and poor, did not. The emperor, whichever one it was, dispatched an agent by the name of Theophilos to arrest the leaders of the persecution at Heliopolis and punish them. In the course of his work, he learned from the guilty parties the names of many of their brethren throughout the whole of Syria and indeed the entire East. The Syriac text of John of Ephesus reports: "They confessed to him about many of their brothers who were in all the land and cities with their names, and also in many of the cities of the Orient, and especially in great Antioch." Which cities were named can now only be surmised, but they must certainly have included the Syrian centers of Greek culture such as Chalcis (Qennishrîn), Callinicum, Edessa, as well as Ḥarrân and other pagan centers denounced by Jacob of Serûg.

As for Antioch, the strength of paganism had been documented only a few decades earlier in the celebrated hearing at Constantinople that brought

---

38. Ibid., p. 100. Moss's translation.
39. See the references above in n. 30. For a discussion of this episode, see G. Downey, *A History of Antioch in Syria* (Princeton, 1961), pp. 563–64.

together pagans from Athens and Heliopolis together with those of Antioch. In the previous century the pagans of Antioch had been so well placed that one distinguished pagan, the sophist Isocacius, was once an intimate of the bishop of the city.[40] The enemies of the Emperor Zeno had even thought it worthwhile to mobilize the pagans in Antioch together with the orthodox Christians in making common cause against the Monophysites. As Glanville Downey rightly observed, it was easy to appeal to the Hellenic heritage "as a means of rallying pagans and classically educated Christians on a patriotic and cultural basis."[41] The mosaics excavated at Antioch with their pagan mythological themes furnish a visual demonstration of the common bond to be exploited between the Christian population and the pagans.

The revelations of the Heliopolitans arrested by Theophilus led to the identification of the pagan high priest at Antioch, a certain Rufinus, as the principal figure in the organization of pagan militants. When the imperial officials went to Antioch to arrest him, it appeared that he had gone to perform sacrifices at Edessa. Finally apprehended there, he succeeded in using one of the sacrificial implements to eviscerate himself in the temple of Zeus and thus to avoid compromising others in what appeared to be a widespread pagan conspiracy.

Nonetheless the imperial enquiry turned up the name of no less a person than Anatolius, the *vicarius* of the praetorian prefect in Edessa, as a participant in the Hellenic cause. Under torture Anatolius implicated the patriarch of Antioch himself and a priest who subsequently became patriarch of Alexandria. He named them as devotees who had joined with him in sacrificing a boy at the shrine of Daphne near Antioch. These revelations understandably caused a storm of controversy in the imperial administration. A trial was held at Constantinople, which ended in the lynching and murder of Anatolius by an angry crowd. The truth, at least where it involves the most highly placed defendants, is still impossible to make out. The Monophysite John of Ephesus was concerned to compromise the memory of the Antiochene patriarch, whereas Evagrius in his *Ecclesiastical History* did his best to exonerate the same man, because he had been his friend and protector.[42]

But the whole affair is a vivid illustration of the strength of Syrian paganism in late antiquity and, in many ways what is more important, the political and social ties of the widely dispersed pagan communities. This would never have been possible if the cults had been confined to local divinities and

---

40. Cf. Downey, op. cit. (n. 39 above), pp. 483–84.
41. Ibid., p. 492.
42. Ibid., p. 564.

celebrated in local dialects. The startling intimations of Christian participation in Hellenism in both its senses at so late a date and at so high a level leads one to suspect that all the mythological mosaics of Antioch and all the Greek secular texts that were circulating now in both Greek and Syriac were more than the harmless and nostalgic accoutrements of a cultured Christian life. Jacob's reply to the spectators at the Greek pantomimes obviously had some truth in it.

On the eve of Islam, Hellenism continued to be a powerful force. Greek-speaking Christians had never been able to set themselves altogether free from it, and Syriac-speaking Christians discovered that they could not exist without incorporating it into their literature and language. This ascendancy of Greek in late antiquity gave new hope to the pagans, while revealing the fragility of the faith of at least some of the Christians.

Despite all this, as has been widely observed recently, the physical traces of Greek culture in Syria tend to disappear in late antiquity.[43] The porticoes, agoras, *bouleutêria*, and theaters can be seen already giving way to the traditional style of a Near Eastern city with its souks before the arrival of the armies of the Prophet. The urban life of the Roman period is distilled under the early Byzantine emperors into a relatively small number of cities that serve chiefly as religious centers. This again shows a concept of the city that is more distinctively Near Eastern than Greek. After all, the very word for "city" in the Semitic languages, *madîna* and related words, derives from a root expressing the administration of justice and the submission to an established order, particularly in religious terms. The word for "religion" in Arabic (*dîn*) appears to be related to the word for "city."

But observations of this kind should not lead to the conclusion that Hellenism in the Near East, and in Syria in particular, was superficial. Quite the contrary. It proved to be very strong, drawing its strength from adapting so flexibly to local tradition. The absorption of Greek models and texts into the Syriac church is only the most conspicuous example of the dissemination of Hellenism within local forms. Something similar may be understood to have given strength and continuity to all the local shrines and cults that proliferated across the varied terrain of Syria from the Mediterranean coast to the environs of the Euphrates. Jacob of Serûg knew whereof he spoke.

---

43. H. Kennedy, "From Polis to Madina: Urban Change in Late Antique and Early Islamic Syria," *Past and Present* 106–9 (1985): 3–27.

IV

Dionysus and His World

In late antiquity the preeminent pagan god seems to have been Dionysus. His nearest competitor for universal recognition was probably Heracles, and it was the extensive legendary travels of these two that underlay their reputation in the remotest parts of the empire. But Dionysus, this god of wine and ecstasy, who had traveled through Anatolia and the Near East to triumph over the Indians, who conversed with other gods as an equal, who was the patron of traveling performers and the mediator of Egyptian wisdom, held pride of place. He was a very different divinity from the classical figure, bearded and serene.[1] The Neoplatonists knew an Orphic tradition according to which Zeus had designated his son Dionysus as king of all the gods of the world down to the sixth generation.[2] For other late pagans Dionysus embodied in himself all the other gods and was at the same time, in his own person, the intelligence of the world. Macrobius makes the interesting distinction, which he borrowed from the Aristotelian physicists, that the world itself was designated Jupiter or Zeus, whereas the intelligence of that world was Dionysus (*Dios nous*).[3] The great pagan holy man of Alexandria, Heraiscus, is even reported to have learned in a dream that he himself had once been Bacchus,[4] another traditional name for Dionysus that remained current in late Greek.

The universality of Dionysus and the innumerable mythologies in which he played a role in the earliest centuries of the Christian empire of Byzantium are exhaustively documented·in the long epic poem by Nonnos of Panopolis, from the mid-fifth century A.D. The forty-eight books of this work, which

---

1. In the catalog of the exhibition *Dionysus and His Circle*, Fogg Art Museum (Harvard, 1979), ed. Caroline Houser, Albert Henrichs gives a valuable survey of Dionysiac images: "Greek and Roman Glimpses of Dionysus," pp. 1–11. At the end of his article, however, he seriously underestimates the character of the late antique Dionysus: "On both levels, the literary and the popular, Dionysus survived for several centuries after Ovid. But as the centuries went by, Dionysus showed increasing signs of wear" (p. 11).

2. Proclus *Comm. in Plat. Cratylum* 5.55.5.

3. Macrobius *Sat.* 1.18.15.

4. Damascius *Vita Isid.* frag. 172, p. 145 Zintzen.

has come down to us under the title of *Dionysiaca*, comprise highly stylized neo-Homeric hexameters devoted to the travels and campaigns of Dionysus. His movement through Asia Minor and the Near East, the cities and places he visited, and the pagan traditions they preserve are chronicled in immense detail. The Indian campaign forms the centerpiece of the epic, but Dionysus's sojourn in Phoenicia is accorded such elaborate treatment that one can only believe that Nonnos had some particular attachment to that region and personal knowledge of it.

Unfortunately the difficulty of Nonnos's Greek and his excruciatingly overwrought descriptions have rarely found favor with modern readers, even though they have engaged the attention of some distinguished philologists. The result is that we have no historical appreciation of Nonnos's great work, even though an excellent critical edition of the text has been available for decades.[5] Nonetheless it has become clear through individual studies of some of the local myths in the poem that Nonnos faithfully reproduces the legends of his own day and that he documents with astonishing precision the way in which indigenous cults were made accessible to a broader public in their Hellenized form. For example, Nonnos mirrors exactly the cults of Phrygian Acmoneia as they can be traced from the coinage of that city, and he reports with equal fidelity the local traditions of Tarsus in Cilicia.[6] The vast treatment given to the city of Beirut, or ancient Berytus, in the *Dionysiaca* reflects the high prestige of that city in late antiquity and its importance as a center of paganism as well as of legal studies.[7] In earlier times Berytus was a city of relatively minor importance.

It is therefore the contemporaneity of Nonnos's poem that makes it so valuable for an understanding of Hellenism in late antiquity. It is no mere exercise in scholarly pedantry, as it is often presented. Since the work itself mirrors, in its colorful Greek, pagan traditions from all over the eastern Mediterranean world—which is, after all, the world of Dionysus—, we must naturally ask where its author belonged in that world. He came from

---

5. The very good edition by R. Keydell is now gradually being replaced by the Budé edition of Nonnos, entrusted to F. Vian, P. Chuvin, and others. A most important book by P. Chuvin, *Mythologie et géographie dans les Dionysiaques de Nonnos de Panopolis*, defended as a thesis at the Sorbonne in 1983, is regrettably still not published. I am deeply grateful to its author for allowing me to read (and make a copy) of the proofs of this work, which the publisher has so far not advanced beyond that stage. This study deserves publication as soon as possible.

6. L. Robert, "Nonnos et les monnaies d'Akmonia de Phrygie," *Journal des Savants*, 1975, 153–92.

7. R. Dostalova-Jenistova, "Tyros a Bejrut v Dionysiakach Nonna z Panopole," *Listy Filologické* 5 (1957): 36–52.

Egyptian Panopolis, a city well known in the fifth century for producing many distinguished pagan poets in the Greek language.[8] Like Alexandria, Memphis, Thebes, Aphroditopolis, Antinoöpolis, and other Egyptian cities of substantial Greek culture, Panopolis also preserved the ancient traditions of Egyptian religion in Hellenic form. If Nonnos has little to say in the *Dionysiaca* about Egypt and its native gods, that should not be understood as showing him less Egyptian or remote from Egypt. On the contrary, it is characteristic of Egyptian Hellenism of the period. This is, after all, an age in which the ancient wisdom of the Egyptian god Thoth circulated in Greek as the revelations of Hermes Trismegistos.[9] What Nonnos tells us about the ancient history of Beirut was similarly transmitted to him through the Greek of Philon of Byblos from an allegedly Egyptian original by a certain Sanchouniathon (who is said to have communicated directly with Thoth).[10]

But we know more about Nonnos of Panopolis. Or at least we seem to know more. A verse paraphrase of the Gospel according to St. John has survived under his name. Although the paraphrase is very much in his style, there are sufficient variations from the Nonnian norms to make some wonder whether or not this is the work of a good, but not perfect imitator. In any case, it would be difficult to believe that anyone who took the trouble to versify the Gospel according to St. John was anything other than a practicing Christian. It has often been assumed that Nonnos converted to Christianity after completing the *Dionysiaca*. The trouble with that assumption is that the Gospel paraphrase seems to show somewhat less metrical control than the *Dionysiaca*, which is supposed to have preceded it.[11] The notion that Nonnos converted to paganism from Christianity after writing the paraphrase has understandably attracted no support.

It is certainly not impossible that a committed Christian could have written the entire *Dionysiaca* and reflected faithfully the mythological traditions of Hellenism in his own day. Christian piety, at least in certain people, was entirely compatible with a profound appreciation of pagan traditions. In the West of the previous century Ausonius is a strikingly good illustration of

---

8. Cf. Alan Cameron, "Wandering Poets: a Literary Movement in Byzantine Egypt," *Historia* 14 (1965): 470–509.

9. G. Fowden, *The Egyptian Hermes* (Cambridge, 1986).

10. Cf. Fowden, op. cit. (n. 9 above), pp. 216–17, with Dostalova-Jenistova, op. cit. (n. 7 above).

11. The matter is still much discussed, in particular by Enrico Livrea, who, with his pupils, is preparing commentaries on individual books of the paraphrase, and by Lee Sherry, who has written a doctoral dissertation on the meter of the paraphrase under the supervision of Alan Cameron.

this.[12] In the century after Nonnos, Dioscorus of Aphrodito brilliantly exemplified the same phenomenon in Egypt itself.[13]

The poem about Dionysus is best read simply on its own terms as an important document of Hellenism and of local traditions in the fifth century. It leaves the reader in no doubt of the universality and omnipresence of Bacchus-Dionysus. After forty-eight books the reader will readily believe that wherever there is religion and myth there is Dionysus. He is in his own godhead the unifying figure of disparate and highly localized cults. He conquers his enemies, and he brings in his triumphant procession salvation to the afflicted. If there is any trace in this work of the Christian empire in which it took shape, it is in the redemptive role of Dionysus. Paganism may be expected once again to have responded to the pressures of Christianity, just as Julian had introduced into his pagan church elements that he had learned from his Christian upbringing—or just as the cult of Korê in Alexandria had absorbed certain distinctively Christian motifs, such as virgin birth or possibly stigmata.[14]

It is well known that Christianity borrowed liberally from the language and iconography of paganism, but it must again be emphasized that this was really a two-way street. Late paganism responded no less to the Christian environment in which it flourished. Neoplatonism, especially of the theurgic or wonder-working kind, was visibly more of a religion than a philosophy. Accordingly we should perhaps acknowledge that at least one line in the *Dionysiaca*, from book 12, could never have been written in a Greek pagan poem before the Christian era: "Bacchus our lord shed tears, so that he might bring an end to the tears of mortals."[15] Pagan gods had certainly not traditionally taken upon themselves the tribulations of mortals. The absorption of Christian elements in late antique paganism, especially soteriological elements, must be carefully distinguished from anti-Christian polemic. Of this there is no trace at all in the *Dionysiaca*.

The Dionysus of Nonnos ranges from small and obscure cults in Anatolian villages to the ancient and time-honored majesty of indigenous gods in great cities. We may profitably look at one illustration of each extreme. A few years ago Louis Robert assembled a group of votive stelae from the

---

12. Cf. G. W. Bowersock, "Symmachus and Ausonius," in *Colloque genevois sur Symmaque*, ed. F. Paschoud (Paris, 1986), pp. 1–15.

13. See now L. MacCoull, *Dioscorus of Aphrodito: His Work and His World* (Berkeley, 1988).

14. Cf. the analysis in chap. 2.

15. Nonnos *Dionys.* 12.171: Βάκχος ἄναξ δάκρυσε, βροτῶν ἵνα δάκρυα λύσῃ.

upper Tembris valley in Anatolia on the border of Phrygia with Lydia.[16] The objects all contained representations of a single divinity with long, curling hair, a beard, and distinctively almond-shaped eyes. He was identified by inscriptions as Zeus Ampeleites. Although the epithet Ampeleites might naturally suggest some association with a vine or vineyard (from Greek *ampelos* for "vine"), the stelae show no representations of vines. Consequently Robert believed that the word did not mean "a guardian of vines" but rather that the Zeus in question was worshipped at a place called "The Vine" or "The Vines." A new representation of this god contains an inscription that describes him as Ampelikos, a form of the epithet that would tend to confirm a reference to a place rather than to the god's role as a protector of vines.

The Ampeleites stelae were distinguished by representations of cows or mares suckling their young. This trademark of the god posed obvious problems of interpretation. Nonnos, however, appears to provide an answer. For among the myths of Anatolia that he reports in the course of Dionysus's progress is a story of how the young Dionysus fell in love with a Phrygian youth whose name was Ampelos. An angry Hera contrived his death by making him ride a bull, which ultimately killed him. Once dead, the boy was metamorphosed into a vine, and hence the explanation of his name as a common Greek noun. This local story of Ampelos and Dionysus, as told by Nonnos, includes a curious detail that would seem to explain the stelae of Zeus Ampeleites.[17] When the bull sprayed Ampelos with water as it was drinking, Nonnos observed that this action looked forward to the time when bulls would toil in a circle around a post to irrigate the vine-planted earth with water. We have here, at last, the necessary connection between Ampelos and Phrygian livestock. This is fundamentally an agricultural myth, and the shrine of Zeus Ampeleites, wherever it was located in the valley of the upper Tembris, reflects that myth.

From the fastnesses of Phrygia we follow Dionysus to the great city of Tyre on the Phoenician coast. Nonnos's lavish treatment of the city is second only in fulsomeness to his account of Beirut. The Tyre to which Dionysus comes in the *Dionysiaca* is not a mythological city lost in time; it is precisely the city created by Alexander the Great and surviving for centuries afterward. It was Alexander who created the causeway that connected the off-

---

16. L. Robert, "Zeus Ampélitès," *BCH* 107 (1983): 529–42, reprinted in *Documents d'Asie Mineure* (Paris, 1987), pp. 373–86.

17. Nonnos *Dionys.* 10.175–12.291. Cf. C. P. Jones, in the catalog edited by S. D. Campbell, *The Malcove Collection* (Toronto, 1985), no. 16, p. 20.

shore islands of ancient Tyre (Semitic Ṣûr) to the mainland. Here is Nonnos's characteristically flamboyant description of the topography:

> He [that is, Dionysus] was delighted to see that city, which the Earth-shaker surrounded with a liquid girdle of sea, not wholly, but it got the shape which the Moon weaves in the sky when she is almost full, falling short of fullness by one point. And when he saw the mainland joined to the brine, he felt a double wonder, since Tyre lies in the brine, having her own share in the land but joined with the sea, which has joined one girdle with the three sides together. Unshakeable, it is like a swimming girl, who gives to the sea head, and breast, and neck, stretching her arms between under the two waters, and her body, whitened with foam from the sea beside her, while she rests both feet on Mother Earth.[18]

Although not an altogether pellucid description of the topography of Tyre, it is clearly the city of Nonnos's own time. The description is supplemented by vivid accounts of the harvesting of purple, for which the city was famous, and the vigorous activity of the ports. Through Dionysus's eyes we also see the streets of the city itself and the precious old buildings that were linked to its past:

> He gazed at the streets paved with mosaic of stones and shining metals, he saw the house of Agenor, his ancestor, he saw the courtyards and the women's apartments of Cadmus; he entered the ill-guarded maiden-chamber of Europe, the bride stolen long ago, and thought of his own horned Zeus. Still more he wondered at those primeval fountains . . .[19]

At this point Nonnos goes on to reveal a detailed knowledge of the city's springs and their names.

In this realistic setting, however baroquely described, Nonnos sets an emblematic encounter of Dionysus with the ancient god of the city, Melqart, traditionally identified with Heracles. Since Heracles himself was a deity almost as popular and widespread as Dionysus himself, it is instructive to read Dionysus's all-embracing invocation of Heracles-Melqart. He is Helios, Belos on the Euphrates, Ammon of Libya, Apis in Egypt, Arabian Kronos,

---

18. Nonnos *Dionys.* 40.311–23.
19. Ibid., 40.354–60.

Assyrian Zeus, Serapis, Mithras, even Delphic Apollo. Heracles' epithet in Nonnos is the remarkable Astrochitôn, "Clothed in a Tunic of Stars."[20] This word, evocative of certain oriental epithets for divinity, appears in Greek otherwise only in the Orphic hymns. This is reasonable enough, inasmuch as much of the invocation of Heracles by Dionysus can be shown to derive from Orphic syncretism.[21] And that in turn calls to mind the Hermetic tracts, also clearly in touch with Orphic traditions. In short, Nonnos gathers up in his verses various traditions of syncretism that were particularly popular and widespread in late antiquity. They served above all to provide a common denominator for the diverse cults of the eastern Mediterranean.

Heracles welcomed Dionysus and offered him a meatless feast of nectar and ambrosia. As the two deities partook of their ethereal dinner, Heracles described the origins of Tyre:

> Hear the story, Bacchus: I will tell you all. People dwelt here once when time, bred along with them, saw the only age-mates of the eternal universe, holy offspring of the virgin earth, whose bodies came forth of themselves from the unplowed, unsown mud. These, by indigenous art, built upon foundations of rock a city unshakeable on ground, also of rock.[22]

Such a foundation legend of autochthonous Tyrians is once again a sign of the astonishing contemporaneity of Nonnos's poem. Older traditions of the foundation of Tyre had brought the settlers there from the Persian Gulf millennia before. Already in book 2 of Herodotus, we have a date of 2750 B.C. for the city's foundation by settlers from the East.[23] This tradition was picked up in the later fourth century by the admiral of Alexander the Great, Androsthenes of Thasos, when he was sailing in the gulf.[24] It was equally known to Strabo in the time of Augustus.[25] In fact, the name of Tyre, *Turos*, was believed to be the same as the name of the island of Bahrain in the Persian Gulf, *Tulos* (where the liquids *l* and *r* are interchanged).[26]

---

20. Ibid., 40.369.

21. Chuvin, op. cit. (n. 5 above), pp. 229–33, has a full discussion, to which I am indebted. On p. 233 he says of the hymn to Heracles Astrochitôn, "tout en étant pétri d'orphisme."

22. Nonnos *Dionys.* 40.429–35.

23. Herod. 2.44. Cf. 7.89.

24. Theophrast. *De causis plant.* 2.5.5; *Hist. plant.* 4.7.7. On all this, see G. W. Bowersock, "Tylos and Tyre: Bahrain in the Graeco-Roman World," in *Bahrain through the Ages: the Archaeology,* ed. Al Khalifa and Rice (London, 1986), pp. 399–406.

25. Strabo 16.3.4, 766C.

26. Cf. Steph. Byz., s.v. Τύρος.

The tradition of the origin of Tyre had thus been deliberately subverted at some time between the first and fifth centuries A.D. It is the new, proud story of autochthonous origins that took over, and it is that which Heracles is made to tell Dionysus. And yet, so exact is the reporting of Nonnos, some hint of the earlier story survives. As we have already observed, Nonnos could not resist telling the reader the names of the springs of Tyre. These are all named for water nymphs, of whom one is a certain Abarbareë.[27] The name is startling, as the names of the other nymphs (Kallirhoê and Drosera) are certainly not: Kallirhoê is simply "The Beautiful Flowing" and Drosera "The Dewy." But what is Abarbareë? Curiously, a nymph of this name appears in the sixth book of the *Iliad* as the mother of an illegitimate child sired by the son of Laomedon at Troy.[28] Nothing in Homer suggests that this nymph was necessarily Trojan, even though her lover was. Nonetheless, it has been customary to distinguish the Homeric nymph from the Tyrian one.

I once suggested that the nymph Abarbareë of Tyre acquired her name from the great god of ancient Tylos, the island of Bahrain from which the earlier tradition claimed the Tyrians sprang. This god was none other than Barbar, whose temple—the temple of Barbar—has been fully excavated in recent times.[29] With a prothetic alpha, Abarbareë makes good sense as a name from the distant past of the Tyrian people. According to Heracles' report to Dionysus, in the early days of the autochthonous Tyrians Abarbareë was, like the other water nymphs, reluctant to take a husband; but Eros reproached her and let fly his arrow, so that Abarbareë and her sisters joined with the sons of the soil to create a divine race of the region. When Laomedon's son met Abarbareë, if she is the same (as, with so odd a name, she ought to be), she was obviously no longer a virgin. But let it be noted, in addition, that in both Homer and Nonnos this nymph is described as a Naiad. In short, what we have in Homer is another mark of the oriental traditions in the *Iliad*, and what we have in Nonnos is a telling name that betrays the novelty of the very foundation story Heracles is telling. Nothing could be more simplistic or foolish than to say that Nonnos has simply lifted, without any further significance, the name of a water nymph from his Homeric prototype.

The confrontation of Dionysus and Heracles over a festive table, so elaborately described by Nonnos, has recently appeared in a magnificent mosaic

---

27. Nonnos *Dionys.* 40.363 and 542–73.

28. Homer *Iliad* 6.22.

29. Cf. Bowersock, op. cit. (n. 24 above), p. 404; E. Weidner, "Ausgrabungen auf Baḥrein," *Archiv für Orientforschung* 17 (1956): 432.

discovered at the city of Sepphoris in Palestine.[30] (PLATE 9.) Dionysus and Heracles at a symposium constitute the central panel of this brilliant floor decoration devoted exclusively to the god of wine. It stands in a building, as yet unexplained, adjacent to the theater of the city. The mosaic, of a date a century or so earlier than Nonnos, is nonetheless full of the spirit of his epic. It shows the universal traveling deity, his triumphant procession (presumably on the way back from India), and his great gift of wine. We see three figures trampling on grapes, and in another panel, candidly entitled Methê (or "Drunkenness"), we see that Dionysus has led his friend Heracles astray: the other great universal god is bending over to vomit into a bowl. There are also representations of the child Dionysus (including what is probably his first bath), and the bringers of gifts to the newborn god. A panel adjacent to the Gift Bringers, or Dôrophoroi, shows three shepherds sitting calmly under a tree.

It is hard not to believe that we have here in visual terms a contamination of Christian elements in pagan mythology such as we have already suggested may be found in the epic on Dionysus. Whatever its exact date and whatever the use of the building in which the Dionysus mosaic occurs at Sepphoris, it is a persuasive confirmation of the importance of this divinity in late antique paganism. The proximity of the building to the local theater may imply, as Homer Thompson has proposed, that this was a base for the traveling performers known as Dionysiac Artists.[31]

More astonishing even than the Sepphoris evidence is the great new mosaic excavated a few years ago by the Poles at New Paphos on Cyprus.[32] Here, as with few other works of late antiquity, we enter completely into the visual and mythological world of Hellenism in both its senses in late antiquity. Dionysus is the controlling figure here. The mosaic consists of six brilliant panels, but it is far more than a simple representation of the god and his exploits. It is a fully developed representation of that pagan revisionism of late antiquity, of which we have seen glimpses in Nonnos and at Sepphoris.

Publishing the mosaic at New Paphos for the first time, the Polish archaeologist Wiktor Daszewski entitled his work, *Dionysos der Erlöser*,

---

30. I am deeply grateful to Eric Meyers, the excavator, for making this material available to me. For a preliminary report, see his article (with E. Netzer and C. L. Meyers), "Artistry in Stone: the Mosaics of Ancient Sepphoris," *Biblical Archaeologist* 50, no.4 (1987): 223–31.

31. H. A. Thompson made this suggestion at a lecture delivered by Eric Meyers at the Institute for Advanced Study, Princeton, on February 5, 1988.

32. W. A. Daszewski, *Dionysos der Erlöser* (Mainz, 1985).

"Dionysus the Redeemer." He could not have chosen a better title to suggest the soteriological aspects of the god. (*PLATES 1–4.*)

There are six panels, of which two depict Dionysus explicitly. One, in the upper right-hand corner, shows the infant god sitting in the lap of Hermes, and the other, in the lower left-hand corner, depicts the triumphal procession of Dionysus, perhaps, as at Sepphoris, on his way back from India. The middle register of the mosaic is devoted to two panels on the same theme, the beauty contest of the Nereids, in which Cassiopeia is seen to be crowned as the victor—much to the annoyance of the Nereids. Beside the panel of the baby Dionysus is a depiction of Leda with a rather dramatic, though scarcely visible, swan; and beside the panel of the Dionysiac procession is a scene showing Apollo sending away the musician Marsyas after his failure to win the competition with Apollo. Observers will know that Marsyas's fate was to be hung upside down and flayed alive. His error is discreetly emphasized by an allegorical figure standing beside Apollo under the designation Planê ("Error").

It is not immediately clear in which direction the mosaic is to be read, although Daszewski has persuasively argued that one should begin in the upper right-hand corner. The placement of Dionysiac panels in the upper right and the lower left would suggest that these are the key places. The infant Dionysus would lead us to believe that we should begin reading there. Hence we end with the triumphal procession of Dionysus. In between we have Leda and the swan, the victory of Cassiopeia, and the defeat of Marsyas.

The two panels on Cassiopeia constitute the most conclusive evidence for the contemporary character of the mythology depicted here. The story of Cassiopeia's rivalry with the Nereids goes back at least as far as Sophocles and had, like the foundation legend of Tyre, a well established classical tradition. That tradition was, quite simply, that Cassiopeia lost in the beauty contest.[33] Poseidon was enraged by the challenge to the pulchritude of the Nereids and wrought his vengeance by bringing a monster out of the sea, before which Cassiopeia's daughter, Andromeda, was ignominiously enchained. What we have in Cyprus from late antiquity is a totally different version of the myth in which this time Cassiopeia is triumphant.

No literary text records the story with this outcome, and it was only

---

33. J.-Ch. Balty, "Une version orientale méconnue du mythe de Cassiopée," *Mythologie gréco-romaine, Mythologies périphériques*, Colloques internationaux du CNRS no. 593 (Paris, 1981), pp. 95–106, with plates following. Also W. A. Daszewski, "Cassiopeia in Paphos—a Levantine going West," in *Acts of the International Archaeological Symposium "Cyprus between the Orient and the Occident,"* ed. V. Karageorghis (Nicosia, 1986), pp. 454–70.

recently that we learned there had ever been such a version at all. In a mosaic excavated at Apamea in Syria just under two decades ago, the contest with the Nereids was depicted with Cassiopeia shown clearly as the winner. The unambiguous evidence of the Apamea mosaic allowed the excavator to show that a mosaic at Palmyra had earlier been wrongly interpreted.[34] It actually depicts the same unusual version of the beauty contest. In the Apamea mosaic, as at Palmyra, the judge is Poseidon, none other than the god who in the standard tradition had taken such a terrible vengeance upon Cassiopeia's daughter. Poseidon there clearly represents the great Semitic god known from several Greek inscriptions in Syria, representing a far more cosmic power than the traditional Greek Poseidon. Yet it was the Greek deity that gave universal expression to the Semitic one. He was in particular the founding god of Beirut.

On Cyprus, as Daszewski has well observed, Poseidon would have been less meaningful. Hence the even more appropriate cosmic divinity, Aiôn ("Eternity"), takes his place as the judge of the beauty contest there. The role is clearly the same, and equally clearly the outcome is the same. What is so remarkable at Cyprus is the framing of the new version—what may be called the Near Eastern version—of the Cassiopeia story within the panels of Dionysus. The victory of Cassiopeia represents the triumph of the gods associated in particular with Cassios, the Mons Cassios in Lebanon, as well as of other divinities rooted in the Near East. The story has been changed, however, not only to elevate a local girl but to demonstrate the suppression of the violent and irrational forces as represented by the Nereids and the monsters of the depths of the sea, depicted in both Cyprus and Apamea. The transformation of the myth is at once local and religious.

That Dionysus should preside over all this is suggested by his role in initiating the episodes—from his infancy on the Cyprus mosaic to his triumph at the end of it. Both the Leda and the Marsyas panels make good sense when interpreted within this concept of the cosmic forces represented by Dionysus. Leda, coupling with the godhead in the form of Zeus as a swan, is explicitly correlated with the power of Dionysus by the figure in a panther skin at the corner of the panel. As we have already seen from Macrobius, Apollo was believed in Neoplatonic circles to be but a manifestation of Dionysus, and the scene depicted in the lower right-hand panel shows the folly of any challenge to divine harmony and order, as represented by Apollo.

The figure of Planê, or "Error," could scarcely be more indicative. Yet

34. Balty, op. cit. (n. 33 above).

Planê is a new allegorical figure to the mythological pantheon. "Error," after all, had been the favored concept of the Christians, as it still is. Deviating or wandering from the path of rectitude is for a Christian often characterized as "error." Until late antiquity, there was no clear path for pagans, because paganism was so fragmented. Its various cults and deities made it almost impossible to wander from any one path. Yet here is "error" in a pagan context.[35] The supremacy of Dionysus suggests a kind of pagan monotheism, responding to Christian monotheism, and with it comes the possibility of error or deviation.

The implicit response to Christianity in pagan motifs here is equally apparent in the panel depicting the infant Dionysus, who sits upon the lap of Hermes, very much like the child on the lap of the virgin. Alongside is the allegorical figure of Theogonia, or "The Birth of God," a pagan Theotokia (to name the equivalent term in Christian texts). Approaching the infant Dionysus in the lap of Hermes are persons holding out their hands in adoration, playing perhaps a similar role to the Dôrophoroi in the Sepphoris mosaic. But here they even more obviously suggest the iconography of the Magi approaching the Christ Child. Dionysus the Redeemer can be seen as an apt description of the Dionysus of the mosaics at New Paphos and as a brilliant exemplification of the new Hellenism.

Since Dionysus characteristically appears in unexpected places at unexpected times, we should not be surprised to find him on another astonishing work of art from late antiquity, only recently made known.[36] (*PLATES 10– 11.*) This is the extensive textile now at the Abegg Stiftung at Riggisberg in Switzerland. Under a series of arches stand figures clearly associated with Dionysiac rites, presumably rites of initiation. Fragmentary pieces from a single textile-hanging in the possession of the museums at Cleveland, Boston, and Riggisberg itself had earlier provided some intimation of representations of this kind.[37] But never before have we been able to see a whole series of figures associated with Dionysus in this format.

---

35. The absence of any pagan personification of πλάνη before the Byzantine age is underscored by the treatment of "error" in the *Tabula Cebetis*, already known in the second century A.D. and perhaps the richest source of personifications: there, at 5.3, a personified ἀπάτη dispenses a drink compounded of πλάνος [*sic*] and ἄγνοια. Cf. J. T. Fitzgerald and L. M. White, *The Table of Cebes* (Chico, 1983). On πλάνη as a personification of "error" in the New Paphos mosaic, see now P. B. Rawson, *The Myth of Marsyas in the Roman Visual Arts, BAR Int. Ser.* 347 (Oxford, 1987), p. 132.

36. D. Willers, *Der Dionysos-Behang der Abegg-Stiftung* (Riggisberg, 1987), a pamphlet distributed with postcards of the hanging. The work measures 730 by 220 cm. I am most grateful to Dr. Willers for personal discussion of the hanging. He will publish a full study of it.

37. Cf. Willers, op. cit. (n. 36 above). Also S. M. Arensberg, "'Dionysus': a Late Antique Tapestry," *Boston Museum Bulletin* 75 (1977): 4–25.

It is too early to speak definitively about the interpretation of the figures, but the Bacchus himself, tipsy and androgynous, is unmistakable. Likewise the Pan figure with his elaborate set of panpipes. Beside him is a mysterious woman with one breast exposed, one bare leg and one covered leg, one bare foot and one foot in a red sandal—provocative to say the least, perhaps lascivious. It would appear that divine figures have a nimbus, although the identification of all of them is not secure. On the other hand, a decently clad, matronly looking woman also has a nimbus, but it is blue, for no obvious reason. A peasant, or at least some rustic figure, seems to be entering the scene, perhaps for an initiation. He is obviously not part of the divine company. Whatever the precise significance of this hanging, it affords a breathtakingly fresh glimpse into the world of Dionysus.

Further revelations about the Abegg Stiftung hanging make this evidence even richer than one had first suspected. Attached to it were a few other scraps of textile. These depict a series of episodes from the New Testament, including Joseph as carpenter, the annunciation to Mary, and Bethlehem. These fragments were reportedly clinging to the Dionysus hanging in such a way as to leave no doubt that they came from the same place, presumably a tomb. We have thus to confront the interesting possibility that all these pieces lay together in the tomb of a Christian rather than a pagan.

Thus the Dionysus hanging and its attached fragments leave us with a problem—or perhaps a solution—very similar to that posed by the *Dionysiaca* epic of Nonnos and the associated paraphrase of the Gospel of St. John.[38] If the textiles both came from the same tomb, we should certainly be prepared to countenance the possibility that the same man wrote those two poems. As Gregory of Nazianzus clearly understood even though he never said so, the Hellenism of Christians could also be no less Hellenic in the sense of "pagan" than it was in the sense of "Greek."

---

38. Note Willers's remark, op. cit. (n. 36 above), pp. 15–16, on the Abegg-Stiftung hanging: "Die ältere Forschung des frühen 20. Jahrhunderts sprach von «hellenistischen» und «späthellenistischen» Stoffen im Gegensatz zu den nachfolgenden koptischen, was wenig glücklich auch heute noch vereinzelt in populären Führen beibehalten wird. Gemeint war seinerzeit allein der «hellenische» Charakter, nicht der «hellenistische» Zeitstil des 3. bis 1. Jahrhunderts v. Chr. Der neue Behang muss also aus der allgemeinen Bildersprache der dionysisch-bacchischen Vorstellungen heraus verstanden und erklärt werden."

V

Greek Literature in Egypt

In the Graeco-Roman world Egypt always seems to be a special case. This is partly due, as the Roman administration quickly recognized, to its economic and strategic importance in the eastern Mediterranean. But the uniqueness of Egypt was due principally to its ancient and highly developed civilization. The extraordinary durability of Egyptian gods, monuments, and styles over several millennia can scarcely be paralleled anywhere else in the whole of human history. Egypt's impermeability in the face of outside onslaughts and influences meant that even as late as the third century A.D. the emperors of Rome could be depicted on temple walls as pharaohs.[1] In Garth Fowden's eloquent phrase, the "airless immobility" of Egypt meant that the Greek culture that flourished there in the centuries after Alexander the Great did not readily join with and reinterpret the indigenous traditions, as it did elsewhere in the eastern empire of Rome.[2]

In a recent review of ethnicity, status, and culture in Ptolemaic Egypt, Roger Bagnall rightly observed that the present consensus that Greeks and Egyptians in that time led parallel rather than converging lives represents a marked change from earlier views.[3] The search for a mixed culture in Ptolemaic and early Roman Egypt proved to be misguided. What can been seen from the Egyptian side during this period, especially in oracular and apocalyptic documents, shows a strong resistance to outsiders. This disposition on the part of the Egyptians was nothing new. Already in the fifth century B.C. Herodotus wrote, on the basis of his personal experience of the Egyptians, "They keep the ancestral laws and add none other. . . . They avoid the use of Greek customs, and generally speaking the customs of all other men."[4] In the Ptolemaic prophecy known as "The Oracle of the Pot-

---

1. At Esna, portraits of Severi: for the problems of Egyptian continuity in the Roman Empire, see F. Dunand, "Culte royal et culte impérial en Egypte: continuités et ruptures," in *Das römisch-byzantinische Ägypten*, Akten des internationalen Symposions 26.–30. September 1978, in Trier (Mainz, 1983), pp. 47–56.

2. G. Fowden, *The Egyptian Hermes* (Cambridge, 1986), p. 63.

3. R. S. Bagnall, "Greeks and Egyptians: Ethnicity, Status, and Culture," in *Cleopatra's Egypt: Age of the Ptolemies* (Brooklyn Museum, 1988), pp. 21–27, esp. p. 21.

4. Herod. 2.79 and 91, elaborated by Fowden, op. cit. (n. 2 above), p. 15.

ter," Egyptians would have found comfort in such words as these: "It will be deserted, the city of foreigners that will be built among us. These things will come to pass when all evils have come to an end, when the foreigners who are in Egypt disappear as leaves from a tree in autumn."[5]

The Greeks and the Romans accommodated themselves to such stand-offishness with remarkable equilibrium. They may simply have recognized that they could do nothing about it. More important, however, was a deep and traditional respect in the Graeco-Roman world for the primacy of Egyptian culture and its pantheon. There was a widespread belief that many of the great gods of Greece had once come from Egypt, and the priests of the Egyptian cults were universally regarded as sages and wise men who had access to the secrets of the universe.[6] Such a regard for the venerable antiquity of the country may explain why it was the only province of the entire Roman Empire in which the standardized iconography of the individual Roman emperors was never imposed. From the Atlantic to the Euphrates, in portraits and statues, Augustus or Trajan or Septimius Severus could be readily identified. But not in Egypt.

Nonetheless the culture of the Greeks and the Egyptians did ultimately begin to merge, largely because Hellenism was both flexible and serviceable, and knowledge of the old Egyptian language and its hieroglyphic script began to die out. Under the Roman Empire it became apparent to the priests of Egypt that they needed Greek to communicate with the rest of the world. They undertook the systematic presentation of oracles and sacred texts in that language to meet the needs of those who could no longer read hieroglyphs. The very exclusivity of the Egyptian priestly class seems to have undermined it in the face of the extraordinary adaptability of Greek language and culture.

By the fifth century A.D. a certain Horapollon, a distinguished pagan, wrote a treatise in two books on the interpretation of hieroglyphic signs.[7] This work presumably was meant to fill a need. Its incompetence in Egyptology is itself an arresting illustration of that need. To keep up appearances, the author is said at the beginning of the work to have written it originally in the Egyptian language, from which it was then translated into Greek. But the wholly Greek representation of the hieroglyphic signs makes this claim more than unlikely. The *Hieroglyphica*, as it is called, is palpably the work of a Hellenic Egyptian who is trying to recover and to understand his own native traditions.

---

5. L. Koenen, *ZPE* 2 (1968): 204–7 (in both Rainer and Oxyrhynchus texts).

6. See the provocative treatment of this ancient belief in M. Bernal, *Black Athena: the Fabrication of Ancient Greece* (New Brunswick, 1987).

7. Horapollon *Hieroglyphica* Sbordone.

Since demotic was not about to fill the intellectual and religious needs of Egyptians, it was thus ultimately Greek, despite long centuries of resistance to assimilation, that became the language in which Egyptians expressed themselves. And it was Greek gods and mythology into which they converted their local traditions without subverting them. Greek, as the language of both Christians and pagans in Egypt, made interaction between the two sometimes explosive, more often creative. It was only with the rise of Coptic Christianity and the vigorous leadership of Shenoute that Egyptian Christianity acquired its own language and could try to separate itself from the ambivalent world of Greek. Coptic provided momentarily for Egypt the kind of nationalist Christianity that Syriac provided for the Christians of Syria and Mesopotamia.

Greek and Coptic Christianity between them encouraged and perhaps explained in part the startlingly rapid Christianization of Egypt in late antiquity. Although recent onomastic studies of the rich repertory of Egyptian nomenclature may be challenged in detail, it now seems clear that on the most conservative estimate well over three-quarters of the country was Christian by the fifth century.[8] But paganism did not die. Students of Neoplatonism have long recognized the importance of the philosophical masters in Alexandria. Still, the recognition of Greek philosophical paganism provides little help in assessing what might have survived of the indigenous traditions in Greek form. The *Hieroglyphica* are rarely mentioned, although its author, Horapollon, came from an important and well-documented pagan family. Confronted with the rapid rise of Christianity and the spread of Hellenism in late antique Egypt, most observers have concluded that Egyptian culture as such simply died. One writer claims that Greek literature of the period almost never mentions Egypt and prefers to concentrate on Greek mythological themes.[9] A new general book on Egypt after the pharaohs even goes so far as to say that paganism, both Greek and Egyptian, survived only in "intellectual and literary circles."[10]

Yet this is hard to credit when one actually looks at the evidence for Egyptian paganism in late antiquity. The Alexandrian rites for Aiôn as celebrated in the shrine of Korê suggest an uncommonly vigorous and evolving paganism.[11] Another example, of a considerably later date, dramatically reinforces this impression. Damascius's account of the burial of the holy

---

8. R. S. Bagnall, "Religious Conversion and Onomastic Change in Early Byzantine Egypt," *BASP* 19 (1982): 105–24. Cf. E. Wypszycka, *ZPE* 62 (1986): 173–81.

9. P. Chuvin, "Nonnos de Panopolis entre paganisme et christianisme," *Bull. de l'Assoc. Budé* 45 (1986): 387–96.

10. A. K. Bowman, *Egypt after the Pharaohs* (Berkeley, 1986), p. 217.

11. See chap. 2.

Heraiscus, a major figure of Alexandrian paganism in the later fifth century, depicts his uncanny closeness to the gods.[12] He was able, for example, to discover which statues of gods were tenanted or inhabited by the deity and which were simple representations that were not living embodiments of the divine. He had only to take a look at an image to fall into a state of physical and spiritual ecstasy, if it were tenanted, whereas, if he suffered no such excitement, there could be no doubt that the god was not present.

It was only to be expected that a man of such uncommon holiness would accomplish something even more remarkable upon his death. As his body was laid out for burial and covered with the linen cloths, there was suddenly a tremendous burst of light. The onlookers were astonished to see divine images depicted on the cloth. This miracle, which has an obvious parallel in the famous Mandylion of Edessa (to say nothing of the Shroud of Turin, which was long identified with it),[13] takes living paganism well beyond a small circle of literary figures.

But since literature is at the heart of the problem of late antique Hellenism in Egypt, it deserves to speak for itself. The literature of the fourth, fifth, and sixth centuries is in fact exceedingly eloquent and by no means in short supply. The splendid achievement of Garth Fowden in elucidating the intellectual and social background of the technical and philosophical works in the so-called Hermetic corpus shows better than anything previously what Greek did for Egyptian traditions.[14] The representation of the Egyptian god Thoth as the Greek Hermes was at least as old as the Ptolemaic period and perhaps much older. The two gods had much in common, particularly the moon, medicine, and the realm of the dead; and, in the Hellenic form in which writings associated with this god were circulated, astrology and mystical philosophy are preeminent. The Hermetic writings purport to be native Egyptian wisdom, rendered accessible through Greek. In the form in which it survives this wisdom presupposes a system of teachers and pupils and not merely individual readers. Its doctrines bear important similarities to the views of the Gnostics. The relation between the two was stunningly confirmed when three Hermetic writings appeared in the treasure of texts in Coptic discovered in the Gnostic library at Nag Hammadi.[15]

Among those three Hermetic works in Coptic is a treatise that circulated in Greek under the title of *Perfect Discourse*. It had been known to scholars

---

12. Damascius *Vita Isid.* frag. 174, ll. 12–17 Zintzen.

13. Averil Cameron, "The Sceptic and the Shroud," inaugural lecture at King's College London, April 29, 1980, published as an independent pamphlet.

14. Fowden, op. cit. (n. 2 above).

15. Cf. ibid., pp. 4–5.

(until the discovery of the Coptic version) in a Latin translation. This work has long attracted attention because of its prophecy of the abandonment of Egypt at a time when the gods would go back from earth to heaven: "A time will come when it will seem that the Egyptians have in vain honored god with pious heart and assiduous devotion, and all holy reverence for the gods will become ineffective and be deprived of its fruit. For god will return from earth to heaven, and Egypt will be abandoned."[16] "God" in the Latin version is *divinitas*, clearly representing the collectivity of pagan gods. This gloomy prophecy of the doom of paganism has often been associated with the destruction of the Serapeum at Alexandria in 392, undoubtedly a traumatic moment for Egyptian pagans. Some have seen the passage as an interpolation in a much older text (which is what the text purports to be anyway), but Fowden has demonstrated conclusively that Lactantius already knew this part of the *Perfect Discourse* at the beginning of the fourth century and quoted it in his own Latin translation made from the Greek he was reading.[17]

Accordingly, the apocalyptic passage can no longer be associated with a particular moment of pessimism among the pagans of Egypt in the late fourth century. It is rather a more generalized prophecy. And as Fowden is alert to point out it is by no means all that pessimistic, since, after the retreat of the gods from earth to heaven, the writer then foretells their coming back to earth: "Those [the gods] who rule the earth will be restored, and they will be installed in a city at the furthest threshold of Egypt, which will be founded towards the setting sun and to which all humankind will hasten by land and by sea." The city would appear to be Memphis. The denouement of the prophecy is thus essentially positive. As Fowden puts it, "The tragedy of Egypt, then, is a parenthesis within eternity, a temporary departure of the gods from earth before the return of the Golden Age."[18] The *Perfect Discourse* takes its place among the positive testimonies of late antique paganism. It does so as an important representative (either real or alleged) of ancient Egyptian tradition.

We do not know when the *Perfect Discourse* in its Greek form ceased to circulate in Egypt. Fowden suggests that its disappearance from the Greek tradition provides a kind of intellectual parallel to the physical violence

---

16. *Asclepius*, in *Corpus Hermeticum*, ed. Nock and Festugière, 2.327.

17. Fowden, op. cit. (n. 2 above), pp. 38–39, citing Lact. 7.15.10 and 7.16.4, translated from the Greek *Perfect Discourse*. For the destruction of the Serapeum in 392, rather than 391, observe A. Bauer and J. Strzygowski, *Eine alexandrinische Weltchronik* (Denkschr. Akad. Wiss.-Wien, Phil.-Hist. Kl. 51.2, 1905), 69 f.—a reference I owe gratefully to Alan Cameron.

18. Fowden, op. cit. (n. 2 above), p. 41.

visited upon Hypatia in the streets of Alexandria in the fifth century. But the accidents of survival are multiform, and we must not forget how very recent is our knowledge of the Coptic version. The existence of the *Perfect Discourse* in three languages in late antiquity tells us enough as it is. It was presumably still available in Greek in the days of Cyril of Alexandria, whose virulent attack on Julian is one of the best proofs of the vigor of Egyptian paganism in the earlier fifth century. Cyril's elaborate reply to the work against Christianity by the long deceased emperor makes frequent reference to Hermes. It includes verbatim transcriptions from works in the Hermetic corpus including the *Perfect Discourse*.[19] Cyril's treatise constitutes a strong reason for not imputing to the pagans of Egypt a sudden paralysis after the destruction of the Serapeum.

In the later fifth century the family of Horapollon, author of the *Hieroglyphica*, comes into full view in the fragments of Damascius's *Life of Isidore*. The family came from the Panopolite nome, well known for Nonnos and other distinguished figures of fifth-century Egyptian paganism.[20] Horapollon's father was an Egyptian priest by the name of Asclepiades, himself the son of the elder Horapollon. The conjunction of Greek and Egyptian theophoric elements in these names describes their religious culture. Asclepiades' brother was none other than the holy Heraiscus, whose burial shroud became emblazoned with divine images when it encompassed his corpse.

Damascius tells us that both Asclepiades and Heraiscus were experts in Egyptian wisdom.[21] Both were evidently priests. Heraiscus appears to have been more holy, Asclepiades better traveled; but both assiduously cultivated knowledge of Egyptian paganism. Asclepiades is said to have been particularly well versed in Egyptian sacred texts. He had studied carefully the traditions of local paganism. He wrote hymns to the gods of Egypt, and he undertook to write a synoptic account of all theologies (obviously all pagan theologies) within the Greek-speaking world. This remarkable undertaking reminds one of Damascius's report that Heraiscus promoted not only his ancestral rites but also those of other countries wherever he could discover them.[22] In fact, a passage in Photius's epitome of Damascius's *Life of Isidore* confirms this interest of the two Egyptian brothers in evidence for cults elsewhere.[23] In Syrian Heliopolis, the modern Ba'albek, Asclepiades is said

---

19. Ibid., pp. 180–82.
20. See the fundamental article by J. Maspero, "Horapollon et la fin du paganisme égyptien," *Bull. Inst. Fr. d'Archéol. Orient.* 11 (1914): 164–95.
21. Damascius *Vita Isid.* frags. 163 and 164 Zintzen.
22. Ibid., frag. 163 Zintzen.
23. Ibid., Photius's epitome no. 94 Zintzen.

to have examined many of the so-called baetyls of the city (the aniconic idols of Semitic paganism) and to have taken an interest in the legends concerning them.

Among Asclepiades' other remarkable literary productions was a history of the earliest traditions of Egypt, stretching back more than thirty thousand years.[24] With such a father, Horapollon was well placed to explore the meaning of hieroglyphs. From both the *Hieroglyphica* and what we can deduce of the works of Asclepiades, the centrality of Greek language and mythology in presenting the ancient Egyptian traditions is absolutely clear. No less clear and no less significant is the effort of both father and son to relate their Egyptian research to the evidence for indigenous cults throughout the Hellenized world. Their work contributes one more important item to the dossier on Hellenism's role in providing a common language and culture to pagans of quite different local traditions.

Another writer from Panopolis of the same period showed a similar broad interest in relating his Egyptian inheritance to his Greek education. This is the political adventurer Pamprepius, whose diplomatic career in Athens and Constantinople came to an unfortunate end after he joined with the conspirator Illous against the Emperor Zeno. As a man of letters, Pamprepius was above all a poet.[25] He sometimes exercised his muse in praise of his foreign patrons, but he never forgot his Egyptian origins. Anonymous verses that survive on a papyrus in Vienna have been reasonably ascribed to Pamprepius and admirably edited recently by Enrico Livrea.[26] We can see there that the poet proclaimed his Egyptian connections. One poem, as we have it, ends with an expression of the writer's wish to return to the muses of Libya and the land of Ptolemy.[27] As an Egyptian pagan Pamprepius seems to have suggested to his highly placed patrons in Constantinople that he might even be able to win over the pagans of Egypt to his desperate enterprise against Zeno. If this is so, it would show clearly that the Egyptian pagans were a constituency worth cultivating.

Among other writers of fifth-century Egypt the same reflection of Egyptian pride in Hellenic terms can be readily discerned. A poem on the rising of the Nile finds room for Dionysus and Orpheus. The praise of Egyptian Thebes invokes Rhea.[28] Perhaps most striking is the fragment of an epic

---

24. Ibid., frag. 164 Zintzen.

25. Cf. Alan Cameron, "Wandering Poets: a Literary Movement in Byzantine Egypt," *Historia* 14 (1965): 470–509. On Pamprepius, *Prosopography of the Later Roman Empire* (Cambridge, 1980), 2:825–28.

26. Pamprepius *Carmina* Livrea.

27. Ibid., p. 31, ll. 197–98.

28. E. Heitsch, *Griechische Dichterfragmente der römischen Kaiserzeit* (Göttingen, 1961), pp. 125–26.

poem on a great battle between the Byzantine armies and the Blemmyes beyond the borders of upper Egypt. This poem, for which we also have an excellent edition from the expert hand of Enrico Livrea, represents a historical event of the early fifth century A.D.[29] Livrea has demonstrated that the author of the poem must have actually participated in the battle and is none other than the great pagan historian Olympiodorus of Egyptian Thebes. The poet decks out the battle with the trappings of the Trojan War and represents it as a great battle of Hellenism over the barbarians. This is at the same time a triumph of Egypt over a hostile and aggressive neighbor.

There is therefore ample evidence of a pagan preoccupation with Egypt in the Greek literature written in late antiquity by Egyptians. It is perfectly true that some works of this period, such as the *Rape of Helen* by Collouthos or the *Capture of Troy* by Triphiodorus, appear to be exclusively versifications of Greek mythology. And even Nonnos's immense *Dionysiaca* is entirely concerned with contemporary Greek mythology outside of Egypt, but we are dealing with a continuum that had purely Greek motifs at one end and purely local at the other. Nonnos himself was proud of his country. He refers to the Nile as "my" river.[30] His interest in other cults does not prove him less Egyptian, but rather more like Asclepiades and Heraiscus—or even Asclepiodotus of Alexandria, who married into an aristocratic family of pagan Aphrodisias in Asia Minor.

Over twenty years ago Alan Cameron called attention to a group of writers whom he identified as wandering Egyptian poets.[31] He brought together an arrestingly large number of figures, including Olympiodorus and Pamprepius, to illuminate what he rightly claimed as an important literary phenomenon in Byzantine Egypt. The survival of Nonnos's vast epic and the clear signs of a swarm of epigones, the so-called *Nonniani*, had obscured the achievements of many other Egyptian poets of the fifth and sixth centuries who, seen as a group, served to certify Eunapius's supercilious observation in the fourth century that the Egyptians "are mad on poetry" (*epi poiêtikêi men sphodra mainontai*).[32]

Cameron began with Eunapius's words and proceeded to put on display dozens of learned and prolific scribblers who exercised their muse in mythological, commemorative, and panegyrical verse. These poets flattered emperors and generals, unearthed or invented traditions about the past that could be useful in the present, and generally offered their services in the

29. E. Livrea, *Anonymi fortasse Olympiodori Thebani Blemyomachia (P. Berol. 5003)*: Beiträge zur klassischen Philologie, vol. 101 (Meisenheim, 1978).

30. Nonnos *Dionys.* 26.238.

31. Cameron, op. cit. (n. 25 above).

32. Eunap. *Vit. Phil. et Soph.* p. 493.

cause of politics and diplomacy throughout the Byzantine East. They wandered, wrote, and prospered. They represented a late antique flowering of a profession that had formerly numbered in its ranks Pindar in classical Sicily, Crinagoras in the court of Augustus, and Pancrates at the side of Hadrian. But posterity thought less well on the whole of these Egyptians, and what survives of their work is but a tiny part of the whole. Fortunately, however, the accidental preservation of poems on papyri helps to provide some measure of the random selection that is essential for a just appraisal of the movement that Cameron uncovered.

A conspicuous characteristic of the movement was its paganism. The poets were almost all pagans; and so when paganism died out in the Thebaid in Upper Egypt, where most of them came from, we are told, in Cameron's words, "Greek poetry died as well."[33] Nevertheless, the wandering poets from Egypt often worked for and praised Christians, taught them, and inspired them in the holy work of composing verse paraphrases of the Old and New Testaments.[34] This posed a problem to Cameron and earlier historians, influenced by the old and unworkable notion of a struggle to the death between paganism and Christianity—a notion implanted and nurtured by the church fathers and until recently part of the conceptual framework within which everyone has examined the centuries after Constantine's conversion.

This notion makes it easy to miss the clear evidence for Christianity in one of the most important of the wandering poets, Cyrus of Panopolis, and to deny the faith of another, who wrote under the transparent name of Christodorus of Coptos. It also forces one to ring down the curtain on the performances of Egyptian poets much too early. By the sixth century Egypt was a thoroughly Christian nation, but Greek poetry had not died. The pagan poetry of sixth-century Christian Egypt has, until just a few years ago, been scorned and neglected. The poet and diplomat Dioscorus of Aphrodito, whose abundant work is preserved on papyrus, fits perfectly with the movement Alan Cameron uncovered in earlier centuries. But even so broadminded a critic of Greek poetry as Denys Page wrote at the front of the volume he contributed to the Loeb Library with translations of Greek literary papyri from classical times to the sixth century A.D., "I have ventured to think that no useful purpose would be served by republishing the fragments of Dioscorus of Aphroditopolis."[35]

In the late 1970s Cameron himself, with the forthrightness and integrity

---

33. Cameron, op. cit. (n. 25 above), p. 508.

34. See M. Roberts, *Biblical Epic and Rhetorical Paraphrase in Late Antiquity*, ARCA 16 (Liverpool, 1985).

35. D. L. Page, *Greek Literary Papyri* (London, 1941), p. v.

that are hallmarks of his scholarship, put the record straight on the faith of Cyrus of Panopolis: "In my study 'Wandering Poets' published in 1965 . . . ," he wrote, "I made the mistake of accepting the allegations of his enemies that Cyrus was a pagan."[36] In several luminous observations Cameron presented a much more subtle and sensitive appreciation of the relation between paganism and Christianity. "There is no need," he noted, "to see 'conflict' or 'tension' between the two worlds." And later he hit the target admirably when he referred to "the common oversimplification of identifying sympathy for classical culture with sympathy for paganism." "It was after all," he declared, "the marriage between Christianity and classical culture . . . that was the defining characteristic and backbone of Byzantine civilization."[37]

It was the art historians who had broken away, well before the political and social historians, from the tendentious historiographical tradition of a life-and-death struggle between Christianity and paganism. Kurt Weitzmann, writing in 1951 in his *Greek Mythology in Byzantine Art*, documents "the insertion of classical figure types, personifications and the like, into Christian scenes." "Such intrusions," he observed, "point to a greater awareness on the part of the artist of the value of the classical heritage. They show his conviction that the latter can be harmonized with the Christian tradition and that both can be amalgamated into a unified style."[38] For Egypt in particular, with the rich art that has been conventionally, if unwisely, labeled Coptic, Du Bourguet remarked many decades ago, before historians took much notice, that the fundamental themes of that art were of pagan origin. Although they were perhaps at the beginning seen symbolically by Christians, they were soon accepted on their own terms without embarrassment. "There was no call," wrote Du Bourguet, "for replacement with other (themes) for the purposes to which they had always been put."[39]

The shared heritage of Hellenism sustained paganism and its symbols. But it also enriched Christianity, just as Christianity transformed late antique paganism. In Egypt the tombs at Hermoupolis Magna, with their frescoes depicting Greek mythological scenes, reveal what Perdrizet has called "the literary baggage of a middle-level bourgeois of Graeco-Roman Egypt."[40] This baggage did not suddenly vanish at the advent of Christian-

---

36. Alan Cameron, "The Empress and the Poet: Paganism and Politics at the Court of Theodosius III," in *Later Greek Literature*, *Yale Classical Studies* 27 (1982): 217–89. The quotation comes from p. 239.

37. Cameron, op. cit. (n. 36 above), quotations from pp. 246, 272, and 287.

38. K. Weitzmann, *Greek Mythology in Byzantine Art* (Princeton, 1951), p. 4.

39. P. M. Du Bourguet, *The Art of the Copts* (New York, 1967), p. 121.

40. P. Perdrizet, *Fouilles de l'Université Fouad à Hermoupolis ouest* (1904), p. 97.

ity. Not for nothing did the family of a wholly obscure person who died at a tender age choose to commemorate him by an inscription that assured other Egyptians that he was adept in Greek literature and sports ("wise in the Muses and a new Heracles"), that he was in fact "a son of Greece" (*Hellados huios*).[41] So eloquent an arrogation of a title that had traditionally been conferred by civic decree evokes the comforting security provided to provincial Egyptians by the images and institutions of Hellenism.

To return to Cyrus of Panopolis: his brilliant career as a poet and as a builder of the Church of the Theotokos in Constantinople, to say nothing of his association with the Empress Eudocia, brought him to the astonishingly lofty eminence of concurrently serving as prefect of Constantinople and praetorian prefect of the East in about 440. He was included in the patriciate and became ordinary consul in 441. He had enemies, as such a man was bound to have, but he turned adversity to success when he won over the notoriously ill-tempered Christians of Cotyaeum in Phrygia to whom he was relegated as their bishop. Timothy Gregory has given us a completely convincing interpretation of Cyrus's brief and famous Christmas sermon to his new constituency in 441.[42] The man was a Christian—perhaps a Christian opportunist, but a Christian all the same. He even dredged up an obscure saint from his childhood at Panopolis to provide a legendary martyr for Cotyaeum, which felt the need of one to enhance its respectability.

Among the undisputed verses ascribed to Cyrus is an encomium to Theodosius II (or possibly an excerpt from a longer panegyrical work):

All the famous deeds of Achilles are yours, except for his wrath and his love; you draw the bow like Teucer, but are no bastard; you have the great beauty of Agamemnon, but wine does not disturb your mind; in prudence I liken you to the cunning Odysseus, but without wicked deceit; and, O King, you distill a honey-sweet speech equal to the old man of Pylos, before you see Time touching the third generation.[43]

All the parallels here come from Homer, and there is a total absence of any reference to the faith of poet or emperor.

A similar point can be made concerning the other uncontested set of verses from the hand of Cyrus. In six lines plausibly alleged by a lemmatist

---

41. E. Bernand, *Inscriptions métriques de l'Égypte gréco-romaine* (Paris, 1969), no. 82: Ἑλλάδος υἱὸν τὸν σοφὸν ἐν Μούσαις καὶ νέον Ἡρακλέα. On "son of Greece," cf. *Bull. épig.* 1966.186.

42. T. E. Gregory, "The Remarkable Christmas Homily of Kyros Panopolites," *GRBS* 16 (1975): 317–24.

43. *Anth. Pal.* 15.9, quoted and translated by Cameron, op. cit. (n. 36 above), p. 229.

to constitute the poet's lament upon leaving Constantinople for Cotyaeum, Cyrus uses pastoral imagery, perhaps Vergilian, to express his dismay over the success of his enemies at court:

> Would that my father had taught me to pasture shaggy flocks, so that, sitting beneath the elms or a rock blowing on my pipes, I might beguile my cares. Muses, let us flee this well built city, let us seek another land; I say to you all that the baneful drones have destroyed the bees.[44]

Once again Christianity does not impinge in any overt way, even though Cyrus is taking leave of the well-built city (parts of which he helped to build) to assume a bishopric in Asia Minor.

Dioscorus of Aphrodito, a prolific poet and diplomat from the sixth century and a Christian resident in a thoroughly Christianized Egypt, is better known to us, thanks to papyri, than most Egyptian poets of the Byzantine period save Nonnos. He gives the lie authoritatively to any suggestion that the end of professed paganism brought with it an end of Egypt's mania for Greek poetry. Modern scorn for the technical weaknesses of his versification tended to keep this important figure out of sight. Hence Page's excluding him from the Loeb Library. He needs to be seen not only in the tradition of Egyptian poets that Cameron identified but as the final proof of the pertinacity and expressive power of pagan myths, gods, and deities in late antique Egypt, when sacrifices were a thing of the past. Even his metrical oddities need to be seen against the changing language of his day.[45]

Were we to have only a few bridal poems (*epithalamia*) by Dioscorus and nothing else, he would undoubtedly have been judged a pagan but for his late date. Here is a specimen for Patricia the pagarch and her Paul:

> Come, Athena, who bravely competed in splendor when Hermes brought two goddesses together: come to sing memories of you. So she cried your song aloud and swore a mighty oath to follow you everywhere, because clearly the mother who bore you was loved by Phaethon, so measureless is your excellence. I call upon your name as most worthy of song of all the daughters of Aphrodito: surely you are full of the beauty of beloved Aphrodite who stands by Love's side: longing has marked your loveliness.[46]

---

44. *Anth. Pal.* 9.36, quoted and translated by Cameron, op. cit. (n. 36 above), p. 231.
45. See now the edition, translation, and commentary for Dioscorus's work in Greek and Coptic in L. MacCoull, *Dioscorus of Aphrodito: His Work and His World* (Berkeley, 1988).
46. Ibid., pp. 81–82.

Or what would an innocent reader conclude from the following Anacreontic verses of this Christian poet?

> I want always to dance. I want always to play the lyre. I strike up my lyre to praise the solemn festival with my words. The Bacchae have cast a spell on me . . . . When I drink wine, my cares go to sleep. What do I care for pains and groans, what do I care for troubles? I love a young soldier, a Heracles with longing eyes, a lion-tamer, even one to save our cities.[47]

It would indeed require the eye of faith to discern a Christian allusion in the Heracles admired here amid dancing and wine, although Heracles is familiar enough in Christian art. Dioscorus, like many contemporary artists, lived unapologetically with these classical figures; and, absorbed into the Christian world, they did not always have to be interpreted symbolically.

It is in the encomia that Dioscorus freely and conspicuously blends Christian and pagan elements in weaving his webs of praise. The poet's earliest work, to an unidentified addressee, displays his characteristic style:

> Sprung from renowned ancestors from the stock of the blessed, from among whom your famous forbear Basil came from God . . . You, too, honored one, have come so like him, exalting the right faith of the Trinity, single in essence. Never, never was there anyone like you in noble birth, quick with every kind of beautiful wisdom. Even when Achilles was dipped in the river he was not equal to your unconquerable self, nor was Telamonian Ajax, nor brave Diomedes.[48]

And so on. The man who spun these verses and cherished the Greek myths without awkwardness or embarrassment was at the same time at home in Coptic, a bilingual product of a bilingual culture. There is no sign of one culture at war with the other any more than of paganism at war with Christianity. The fabric was intricate but whole.

The poets and artists of Egypt held on to the gods and heroes of the pagan past not to protest anything that went on in the present. This is clear enough from their invocation of those gods and heroes to extol the present. It is far more likely that the tenacity of Hellenism in late antiquity should again be viewed as the means by which a people could retain their hold on their own

---

47. Ibid., pp. 119–20.
48. Ibid., pp. 63–64.

local identity in the face of a universalizing religion. The Greek myths linked them with their forebears and with a common education their ancestors had shared for centuries. Conversion did not demand a renunciation of the past.

Not for nothing did the Egyptian poets include in their oeuvres, in addition to panegyrics, commemorations of battles, celebrations of marriage, and pen portraits, versified histories of cities that traced their origins to legendary founders. This part of the work of the poets has been too little appreciated because virtually none of it survives in its original form. But we know it was there in abundance. Christodorus of Coptos, represented in extant literature exclusively by his descriptions of statues in the gymnasium of Zeuxippus in Constantinople, was the author of local histories (*patria*) of six cities—Nacle, Thessalonica, Miletus, Tralles, Aphrodisias, and (at great length) Constantinople.[49] Similarly, a poet called Claudian, writing in Greek but unlikely to be identified with the famous Latin poet from Egypt, is known to have specialized in the composition of *patria*, including works on Nicaea, Tarsus, Anazarbus, and Berytus.[50] These poems were the successors of foundation poems (*ktiseis*) from the classical and Hellenistic ages, but the passion for them in late antiquity suggests a renewed enthusiasm for tracing roots in the mythical past through pagan genealogies and legends.

Although the foundation poems of Christodorus and Claudian are lost to us, the attentive reader of Nonnos's *Dionysiaca* will be conscious of their presence in his accounts of the cities and regions through which Dionysus traveled. The *Dionysiaca* may well conserve for us the substance of many of those lost *patria*. Not the least of Nonnos's merits is the proof he gives of pagan stories in an increasingly Christian world as a vindication of local traditions. Similarly, excavations may uncover more pointers to the lost *patria* of late antiquity. The recently published reliefs from the Sebasteion at Aphrodisias, with their images of the city's legendary founders, may reflect the stories that Christodorus later included in his attested poem on Aphrodisias, a city that had drawn several of Egypt's most celebrated pagan holy men to its gates in late antiquity.[51]

It was this use of Hellenism as a link with the past and as a guarantee of local cultures that made the early Byzantine poets, both Christian and pagan, so firm in their hold on Greek mythology. Appropriately enough the interpretation that I am suggesting here was expressed in lapidary fashion by a modern Greek poet from Egypt whose intuition was uncannily sound.

---

49. *Prosopography* (n. 25 above), p. 293.

50. Lemma on *Anth. Pal.* 1.19. Cf. Cameron, op. cit. (n. 25 above), p. 490.

51. R. R. R. Smith, "The Imperial Reliefs from the Sebasteion at Aphrodisias," *JRS* 77 (1987): 88–138.

Like certain of his antecedents in the fifth and sixth centuries, Constantine Cavafy was himself a Christian. This is what he wrote:

That we've broken their statues,
that we've driven them out of their temples,
doesn't mean at all that the gods are dead.[52]

---

52. C. P. Cavafy, *Collected Poems*, ed. G. Savidis, trans. E. Keeley and P. Sherrard (Princeton, 1975), pp. 62–63 ("Ionic"). Paul Zanker has pointed out to me that the destruction or mutilation of pagan statues implies in itself a lively belief in the power or "numinosity" of those statues. For an excellent discussion of Christian and pagan views of animate statues, see the forthcoming article by H. Saradi-Mendelovici, "Christian Attitudes towards Pagan Monuments in Late Antiquity and their Legacy in Later Byzantine Centuries."

VI

Hellenism and Islam

The rise of the Prophet Muḥammad in the seventh century A.D. and the extensive Muslim conquests that followed the proclamation of Islam as a pan-Arab faith must be reckoned, on any accounting, among the most significant events in the history of the world. The religious affinity provided to tribal peoples of great diversity transformed the hegemony and society not only of the Near East but of North Africa, Spain, and Southeast Asia. The consequences of the Islamic revolution are clearly with us today, in some ways more than ever. The reasons for the success of Muḥammad and his faith are neither simple nor obvious. Historians have long tried to juggle in their assessments the charismatic leadership of the Prophet, the spiritual receptivity of his people, and the inherent weaknesses in the Byzantine and Persian empires.

There seems, however, to be general agreement that the Muslim armies were able to achieve such rapid success after the Prophet's death in part because the Hellenization of the Near East had been essentially superficial. It could therefore provide no substantial resistance. The spectacular defeat of Heraclius in 636 at the Battle of the Yarmûk seemed to represent a collision of cultures. The Byzantine troops were engaged in an unfamiliar terrain: the Yarmûk wadi symbolized the Syrian countryside and indigenous Semitic traditions, among which the Byzantine forces were helpless. In his pioneering and still fundamental *History of the Arabs*, Philip Hitti wrote, "The Hellenistic culture imposed on the land since its conquest by Alexander was only skin-deep and limited to the urban population. The rural people remained ever conscious of cultural and racial differences between themselves and their masters."[1] The same sort of thing can be found as recently as 1981 in Fred Donner's important study of the early Islamic conquests. According to Donner, "The Hellenistic impact on Syria was, however, always a bit artificial, and Hellenistic culture always something imposed on Syria from above. Even after nearly ten centuries of exposure to Greek language and

---

1. P. Hitti, *A History of the Arabs* (London, 1970), p. 153.

Graeco-Roman culture, the great mass of the Syrian populace remained thoroughly Semitic." He goes on to say, "Among the great masses in Syria who could neither read nor write, Hellenism had sent down only very shallow roots before striking the solid Semitic bedrock."[2]

There is both factual and conceptual error in opinions such as these. It is simply wrong, as we have seen, to maintain that Hellenism in Syria, or in the Near East more broadly understood, was confined to the cities. Obviously the high culture of Greek rhetoric, philosophy, and law was centered in the major cities, just as high culture normally shows up as an urban phenomenon in any state or society. But the use of Greek as a language, however corrupted into local dialects, and the adaptation of Greek myths, gods, and images for local purposes were an integral part of rural paganism throughout the Near East. The misconception of Hellenism as an urban phenomenon rests very largely on the failure to explore the multivalence of the word Hellenism (*Hellênismos*), its designation of "paganism" in general as well as Greek culture both Christian and pagan. It was with reference to paganism that it was particularly applicable to the countryside, as local cults and local burial places attest. The Greek pantheon gave strength to rural pagans by serving as a paradigm of polytheism and by representing obscure and unfamiliar deities in the universally recognizable forms of Greek mythology.

But the real problem in the simplistic view of the superficiality of Hellenism in the Near East is conceptual. There is an unspoken presupposition that Hellenism and what Donner calls "Semitic bedrock" are fundamentally incompatible. And yet it is clear that what gave late antique paganism its strength and coherence was the extraordinary flexibility of Greek traditions themselves in responding to local needs. At the local level Greek culture provided a means of expression to indigenous peoples as well as a pagan model. Without the common denominator of assimilation into Greek deities, the Egyptian poet Nonnos would have been unable to broadcast the exploits of the "god of the Arabs" or of Melqart, the ancestral god of Tyre.

The rural Christians, no less than the pagans, made use of Greek mythological iconography to adorn both their churches and their homes with mosaics that evoked, in a reassuring and still meaningful way, the old local cults of the region. So in the Church of the Virgin at Mâdabâ in Jordan we find an elegant representation of Aphrodite, the Greek form of the ancient Arab goddess al-ʿUzzâ, or in the Church of the Apostles a portrait of the goddess Tethys symbolizing the sea, with her right hand raised in that characteristic gesture associated with a Semitic pagan divinity.[3] Such scenes

---

2. F. M. Donner, *The Early Islamic Conquests* (Princeton, 1981), pp. 92 and 94.

3. See F. Zayadine, "Peintures murales et mosaïques à sujets mythologiques en Jordanie," in *BCH* Suppl. 14, *Iconographie classique et identités régionales* (Paris, 1986), pp. 407–32. See

provided a local habitation for the universalizing Christian religion without compromising it. In short, for both pagans and Christians alike in the Near East, Hellenism was not something different from the Semitic bedrock: it *was*, in a certain sense, the Semitic bedrock.

It is perfectly true that, when the Arabs heeded the call of Muḥammad in the seventh century, the high culture of Hellenism had few strong roots in the eastern Mediterranean outside the major cities, especially those on the coast. Many of the great colonnades and agoras had disappeared. The Neoplatonists of Qennishrîn and Apamea had died out. But the legacy of Hellenism in other respects was stronger than ever and contributed to creating the foundations of Arab nationalism upon which Muḥammad was to build.

In many ways Hellenism prepared the way for Islam by bringing the Arabs together and equipping them with a sense of common identity. At the beginning the pagan pantheon of the Arabs had been very small. Herodotus was aware of two divinities, who were essentially a god and his consort.[4] By the time the Prophet arrived in Mecca in 630, he was able to destroy 360 different idols of Arab paganism.[5] The proliferation of Arab gods and goddesses was a direct response to the polytheism of the Greeks. The worship of these deities at international festivals, held on a regular basis, was borrowed directly from the tradition of fairs and festivals celebrated by the Greeks.[6] In the best Hellenic tradition, these pagan festivals of the Arabs included a statutory truce among all participating tribes. Nonnosos, an Arabic-speaking diplomat at the court of Justinian, reported in detail and in Greek to the Byzantine court on the festivals and cultic observances of the Arabs.[7] These were, as he knew, indigenous ceremonies that would be understood in Constantinople because the very traditions of Constantinople had been their model.

As Toufic Fahd, the best modern chronicler of the pre-Islamic Arabian pantheon, has observed, Hellenism, with its myths, rites, and mysteries, introduced into the theodicy of Semitic paganism numerous elements that could potentially corrupt its purity and falsify its perspectives.[8] It was per-

---

fig. 14 for Aphrodite in the Church of the Virgin and fig. 13 for Tethys in the Church of the Apostles.

4. Herod. 3.8.3.

5. Ibn al-Athîr *Kâmil* 2.192.

6. See the discussion in chap. 3.

7. Nonnosos, *FHG* Müller 4:179–80.

8. T. Fahd, *Le panthéon de l'Arabie centrale à la veille de l'Hégire*, Inst. fran. d'arch. de Beyrouth, Bibliothèque arch. et hist. vol. 88 (Paris, 1968), p. 253. For the use of statue types associated with the eastern imperial cult as models for representations of kings in Yemen in the late third century A.D., see the two extraordinary bronze statues discussed by K. Weidemann in *Könige aus dem Yemen: zwei spätantike Bronzestatuen* (Mainz, 1983), a publication of the

haps to protect the Arabs from an excessive transformation of local paganism on the Hellenic model that the organization of the pantheon was re-
formed and its observances codified in the third century A.D. by a certain
'Amr ibn Luḥayy. It would seem that the carefully elaborated language for
distinguishing iconic from aniconic representation of the gods was then first
worked out, to be perpetuated in Muslim historiography later.[9] But at the
same time the normalization of cults represented a pan-Arabism that was
quite new to the Near East. It mirrored, in fact, the pan-Hellenism that had
for so long kept all peoples of Greek culture in touch with one another.
Without the cohesion fostered by the religious observances of the pagan
Arabs in late antiquity, it is arguable that the Prophet would have had no
audience for his great message.

In recent years the most arresting illustration of Hellenism in the service
of indigenous Arab culture has been the excavation of the city of Faw in the
interior of the Arabian peninsula. The work has been carried out by the King
Saud University of Riyadh under the able direction of 'Abd al-Raḥman Al-
Anṣary.[10] The site of Faw lies on the route north from Mârib in the south
through Najrân to al-Yamâma. It would have been traversed by traders
going to and from the Persian Gulf as well as to and from Transjordan along
the route that joined Hâ'il with al-Yamâma. The city lay at the center of the
famous kingdom of Kinda, known from literature to have been situated in
just this area. As a result, this single excavation has transformed the name of
Kinda from a name in literary texts into brilliant reality. Its buildings, paintings, sculpture, coins, and pottery illustrate a prosperous urban environment, and its graffiti and inscriptions show that this was a literate society.
Inscriptions at Faw were written in the Musnad script that served equally for
the south Arabian kingdoms and for the caravan traders and bedouin who
traversed the northern desert all the way into southern Syria. Although the
language has hitherto been best known from texts in the south, the variety
found at Faw shows distinctive features of northern grammar and traces of
the emergent Arabic language, which the local citizens may well have spoken among themselves.[11]

The inscriptions show that we are dealing with a thoroughly Arab society.
The gods that they commemorate show equally an exclusively Arabian pan-

---

Römisch-Germanisches Zentralmuseum. Note especially pp. 21–22. I am very grateful to Paul
Zanker for drawing my attention to this publication.

9. Fahd, op. cit. (n. 8 above), pp. 250–51.

10. A. R. Al-Anṣary, *Qaryat al-Faw: a Portrait of Pre-Islamic Civilization in Saudi Arabia*
(Riyadh, 1982).

11. Ibid., p. 28.

theon. Allât, al-'Uzzâ, Manât, and Shams take their place alongside attestations of these divinities throughout other parts of the Arab world in the centuries before the Prophet. There is a special deity of the city, Kahl, who is new to history. The Arab character of the population is unambiguously documented in theophoric names such as 'Abd al-'Uzzâ and 'Abd al-Shams, "The Slave of al-'Uzzâ" and "The Slave of Shams."[12]

Much of what survives in this indisputably Arab city of the Hellenistic and Roman periods may actually be contemporaneous with the alleged reforms of 'Amr ibn Luḥayy in the third century A.D. (*PLATES 12–14.*)

The wall paintings of Faw have produced one of the most haunting images of the Roman/Byzantine East to have come to light in modern times. An eminent local citizen is being crowned by two young persons, one on either side. His head is being draped in grapes, of which a large bunch is suspended over him. His face is round with large bulging eyes and a drooping moustache. His name, written in the Musnad script to the side, is the good Arab name of Zaki. These representations, in a society to which anthropomorphism was fundamentally alien, dramatically demonstrate the extent of Hellenic influence. Here, as earlier in Nabataea to the north, anthropomorphism had been taken over from the Greek tradition, but the faces and figures are distinctively local. The bunches of grapes are undoubtedly another Hellenic touch, a reflection of the ubiquitous and widely assimilated god, Dionysus. The whole idea of honoring a local notable in this way, with attributes that are evidently divine and with figures who may well be in priestly robes, is nothing less than an Arab transformation of the Hellenic institution of *euergesia*— "public benefaction" with all the attendant honors lavished upon the benefactor by his city. Yet the face, the figures, the Musnad script, and the name are all unmistakably Arab. Here in the center of the Arabian peninsula Hellenism inspired a hitherto unsuspected commemoration of local prosperity and culture.

Equally startling is the appearance of the Graeco-Egyptian god Harpocrates with a double crown on his head. His presence at Faw may perhaps reflect the trading activity of the city, but equally it could evoke a syncretistic subculture of Greek late antiquity, as best known to us in the Hermetic treatises. Whatever the correct interpretation of this figure, it draws the city of Faw into the orbit of Hellenic paganism. Yet nonetheless the city preserved everywhere its fundamentally Semitic character; its graffiti are as eloquent as its inscriptions.

The Hellenism of Faw prefigures the growth of Arab paganism in the

---

12. Ibid.

three centuries between 'Amr ibn Luḥayy and the Prophet. It consisted in the anthropomorphic polytheism of Faw's pagans, but it was not a Hellenism in the sense of using the Greek language or of assimilating all deities to Greek ones. The Greeks would undoubtedly have been hard put to match the 360 gods that were worshipped when Muḥammad went to Mecca in the seventh century. But Hellenism had played its irrevocable part in assisting the Arabs to discover a sense of their own national identity.

In the more northerly parts of the Near East, the Greek language itself had served as a bridge when Palmyrene and Nabataean declined. Although Syriac prospered among the Christians, its identification with the Church rapidly made it inappropriate for the pagans. Arabic, which had probably been spoken for centuries even though it was rarely written (even in the days of the Nabataeans and the Palmyrenes), only gradually took over as the common language that bound the Arabs together. Its first appearances in writing, on a graffito in Nabataean letters of the first or second century A.D. and again in an inscription in Nabataean letters of the fourth century A.D., provide precious clues to the spread of spoken Arabic in the first three centuries of the Roman Empire.[13]

The use of Arabic in late antiquity at cult centers such as Petra, and presumably at the sixteen pilgrim fairs mentioned by the Arabic sources, shows that the Arabs' common language was at last becoming an instrument that could be used for some high purpose. The great shaikhs at the courts of the Arab confederacies of the Ghassanids and the Lakhmids, who constituted the principal Arab allies of the Romans and the Persians respectively, provided congenial environments for some of the earliest known poets in classical Arabic.[14] The odes they composed for their princely patrons, largely on military and erotic themes, were known to the Greeks and described by the Greek word *ôidai* ("odes").[15] It would not be at all unreasonable to suppose that the emergence of Arabic court poetry was inspired by the Hellenic model in the same way as the cultivation of anthropomorphic gods. Certainly, in Semitic terms pagan Arab poetry is in its complexity and rhythmic virtuosity the equal of the great Christian hymns in Syriac by Ephraem. Although both Syriac and Arabic are Semitic languages, outside

---

13. A. Negev, "Obodas the God," *IEJ* 36 (1986): 56–60 (graffito of first or second century); J. A. Bellamy, "A New Reading of the Namârah Inscription," *JAOS* 105 (1985): 31–48 (most recent publication of the fourth-century inscription).

14. Cf., for a general introduction, H. Gibb, *Arabic Literature* (Oxford, 1966), pp. 13–31 ("The Heroic Age").

15. Sozomen *Hist. Eccles.* 6.38: παρὰ δὲ Σαρακηνοῖς ἐν ᾠδαῖς ἐστιν.

traditions impelled them both to new eloquence. In the sense in which it may be said that Ephraem's hymns were Christian, the Arab odes were Hellenic.

In a recent and powerful study Patricia Crone has challenged the notion, tenaciously held until now, that Mecca and the family of Muḥammad derived their strength and influence from extensive trade.[16] This means that the mercantile origins of the Islamic revolution in the seventh century must probably be abandoned, or at least given far less weight. The removal of commerce from our understanding of the rise of Islam opens up to clearer view the enormous role that Arab paganism played in bringing together the disparate tribes, precisely as the growth of the Arabic language enabled them to communicate more easily with one another. Because Greek practices had helped the Arabs to find their identity in the centuries before the Prophet, it should now be less surprising that some of those practices persisted conspicuously after the Prophet's death. It was not only that old ways die slowly: it was that the new ways had, in important respects, their roots in the old ones and could therefore scarcely be expected to eliminate them overnight.

The Greek language itself held on tenaciously under the early Umayyad caliphs in areas where it had not already been supplanted by Arabic before the arrival of Islam. In other words, Arabic prospered where it had already prospered before Muḥammad, whereas Greek was taken over as the language of the Muslim bureaucrats where it had been the standard language before them. The papyri from the little town of Nessana in the Negev Desert are the principal illustration of such persistence of Greek under the Umayyads. They show the use of the language to the end of the seventh century, not only, as might be expected, among the Christians of the town, but equally among the bureaucrats employed by the caliph at Damascus. A shortage of Arabic scribes cannot be the explanation of this phenomenon. Some documents, notably the requisitions known as *entagia*, are bilingual in Greek and Arabic.[17] Yet none is uniquely in Arabic.

Perhaps the most striking of the Nessana papyri is a long text that emanates from the highest level of Umayyad officialdom, making reference to the celebrated caliph at Damascus, 'Abd al-Malik, who ruled at the end of the seventh century.[18] The papyrus, a record of accounts involving orders from

---

16. P. Crone, *Meccan Trade and the Rise of Islam* (Princeton, 1987).

17. C. J. Kraemer, *Excavations at Nessana*, vol. 3, *Non-Literary Papyri* (Princeton, 1958). The *entagia* comprise nos. 60–67, pp. 175–97.

18. Ibid., no. 92, pp. 290–99.

both Damascus and Egypt, is entirely in Greek, although replete with Arabic names and words. It makes reference to institutions of the Muslim army, such as rations of food (*rizq* in Arabic), represented in Greek as *rhouzikon*, as well as to cash allowances called *rhoga* in Greek, corresponding with an Arabic calque (in this case *raj'a*). 'Abd al-Malik himself is named in Greek as Abdelmalech, and he bears in Greek letters the designation Amir al-Moumnin, "Lord of the Believers." All the personal names in the document are Arab names. But the accounting procedures and terminology are Greek throughout.

The document mentioning 'Abd al-Malik can be dated to about 685. It is among the last of the Nessana papyri. The naming of 'Abd al-Malik in a Greek document has more significance than might at first appear, for it was this caliph who took formal steps to put an end to the use of Greek in the Muslim bureaucracy. He—or according to some sources his son—called for the language of the public registers (*dîwân*) to be changed henceforth from Greek to Arabic. He seems equally to have been responsible for the creation of a genuinely Arabic coinage.[19] The Umayyads had relied hitherto on Byzantine coin types. The Arabic writer al-Balâdhuri explains the mandatory change from Greek to Arabic as a reaction to an unfortunate incident in which a Greek scribe urinated into an inkwell.[20] The real reason must evidently be that the use of Greek in areas where it still survived showed no signs of yielding on its own to Arabic.

Undoubtedly in the fullness of time, even without the impetus provided by 'Abd al-Malik, Arabic would probably have spread just as it had previously in Syria, Jordan, and the Peninsula. Less easily eliminated were the nonlinguistic traces of Hellenism to which the Umayyad rulers were heir. In a strong reaction against the Hellenized anthropomorphism of the Arab pagans, Muḥammad had strictly forbidden his followers to depict the human face or form. The intricate decorative patterns of early Islamic art are an obvious response to the Prophet's prohibition. It was a deliberate repudiation of the Hellenic past and, in a monotheistic setting, a return to the nonrepresentational devotions of the earliest Arab tribes. Nothing could have been more surprising, therefore, to students of early Islam than the discovery, toward the end of the last century, of a cluster of Umayyad buildings containing on the walls of a bath representational paintings of the most cheerful and abandoned sensuality.

The building, known as Qaṣr al-'Amra, appears to have been a kind of

19. Cf. Hitti, op. cit. (n. 1 above), p. 217.
20. Al-Balâdhuri *Futûḥ al-buldân*, p. 193.

desert retreat for jaded princes and superior administrators.[21] Within a century or so of the Prophet's death these Muslim leaders evidently took pleasure in relaxing amid illustrations of naked women, lively and benevolent animals, and scenes from Greek mythology. The Hellenic inspiration of the decorations on the walls of ʿAmra is underscored by the Greek names attached to certain of the figures shown. In this beguiling desert chateau there is little sign, apart from the architecture of the buildings themselves, that the region is now firmly in the hands of an Islamic administration. (PLATE 15.)

The paintings do not show any trace of embarrassment. They are certainly not pornographic, but they are exuberant. They are undoubtedly inconsistent with the tenets of Islam, but they are fully consistent with the cultural inheritance of the region. If this kind of thing had been an alien accretion in the Near East, like the colonnades and agoras that had disappeared long since, it would not have reappeared under the Umayyads. What we see at ʿAmra is an indigenous Hellenism that is local, not alien. The Dionysus that appears on the walls of ʿAmra is the Arab Dionysus of the Nabataeans, the Dionysus whom Nonnos brought to Arabia, and the Dionysus of the Sepphoris mosaic. ʿAmra is neither a sign of Muslim toleration nor of secret and forbidden pleasures. It is simply a sign of the Muslims' own world.

Oleg Grabar, the most acute and subtle of all the interpreters of the ʿAmra paintings, has stunningly confirmed the local character of its motifs in a recent study of the hunting scenes.[22] He points out that four separate scenes, including a butchery, depict what appear to be wild horses and wild cattle. In substance and form Grabar can find no parallel to these images at ʿAmra in the huge repertoire of hunting scenes in the ancient world. There is nothing comparable at Piazza Armerina, Constantinople, or the palaces from Spain to Syria. But each of the scenes can readily be explained in terms of the nomadic culture of the region. Early Arabic poetry provides parallels for the wild cattle. In Grabar's words, "The specificity of the image and the quasi-automatic possibility of situating the event depicted within the immediate context of the representation renders superfluous any external model. One can go further and suggest that in each case it is a concrete and local event that is represented."[23] The true character of the ʿAmra paintings, in

---

21. M. Almagro et al., *Qusayr ʿAmra* (Madrid, 1975). Cf. F. Zayadine, "The Frescoes of Queseir ʿAmra," *Archaeology* 3 (1979): 19–29.

22. O. Grabar, "La place de Qusayr Amrah dans l'art profane du Haut Moyen Age," *Cahiers archéologiques* 36 (1988): 75–83.

23. Ibid., p. 81.

which a Greek visual language is employed to commemorate an Arab way of life, could not be better described.

Christians under the Umayyad caliphs might more naturally be expected to have persisted in the use of Greek where Syriac was not spoken, at least until the dissemination of the Bible and other sacred texts in Arabic. But the discovery a few years ago of a church at the site of Umm er-Reṣâṣ in Jordan went far beyond what anyone had expected. A mosaic inscription, written in Greek, is dated clearly to the year 785.[24] That means it belongs no longer to the Umayyad caliphate but to the time of the Abbâsids, who came to power in 750 and ruled from Baghdâd. We are well beyond the early days of Islam. The dating of the text is, moreover, according to the years of the province of Arabia, a system of reckoning that one would have thought had disappeared along with the Roman and Byzantine province that it named. Even more remarkable than the text is the series of illustrations that accompanies it. The mosaic contains a series of carefully designed illustrations of the great cities of the Near East.[25] The schematic representations are reminiscent of the famous mosaic map at Mâdabâ of a considerably earlier date.[26] But here there is no map, only the schematized depictions of the cities with their identifications, again in Greek. (*PLATE 16.*)

At Umm er-Reṣâṣ we have a form of mosaic that represents the best of Greek traditions of several centuries before. This work appears in a context dated toward the end of the eighth century by the year 680 of the province of Arabia—when there was no province of Arabia. Nothing could be more startling, or more revealing. The mosaic at Umm er-Reṣâṣ shows more eloquently than anything hitherto that the Hellenism of this part of Jordan was deeply rooted and expressed a local pride. There is nothing superficial about it. It is part of the bedrock. If it were not, it would certainly not have survived after a century of Islamic rule. The representation of the cities, by this means and with their Greek names, helped in the late eighth century, as it had in earlier times, to provide a sense of the community of the inhabitants of the eastern cities. The cities appear to be identified not so much by the representation of churches as ecclesiastical centers but by the reference to the most conspicuous buildings that would distinguish one urban center from another.

---

24. M. Piccirillo, "Le iscrizioni di Um er-Rasas—Kastron Mefaa in Giordania I (1986–1987)," *Liber Annuus* 37 (1987): 177–239. The text dated to 785 is no. 4, presented and discussed on pp. 183–86.

25. Cf. the undated brochure by M. Piccirillo, *Um er-Rasas Kastron Mefaa in Giordania* (Jerusalem), published by the Franciscan Printing Press.

26. H. Donner and H. Cüppers, *Die Mosaikkarte von Madaba*, Abh. des Deutschen Palästinavereins (Wiesbaden, 1977).

The papyri at Nessana, the chateau at 'Amra, and the mosaic floor at Umm er-Reşâş all point to a remarkable continuity of Hellenism in both its cultural and pagan aspects. This is in no way a repudiation of the momentous changes wrought by the Prophet and the conquests of the early Islamic armies. Quite the contrary: it is proof of the indigenous character of Hellenism in that part of the new Islamic world, and it is proof that at least some of the roots of Islam were embedded in that local Hellenism.

But even as the Abbâsids consolidated their hold on the bureaucracy and culture of the Near East, the Arab scholars in Baghdâd began gradually to realize how much they needed to learn from the Greeks. Under the leadership of a certain Ḥunain ibn Isḥâq, they undertook a prodigious program of translations of the great Greek classics, particularly in philosophy and medicine, into Arabic (sometimes by way of Syriac versions).[27] This infusion of Greek culture of a kind that was palpably not local came hard on the heels of the disappearance of the traditions we have examined here. Ḥunain and his colleagues were concerned with Greek high culture and absorbed it out of the same sense of need that had driven the early Syriac church to resort to wholesale translations many centuries before.

The story of the Arab transmission of Greek texts, many of them now lost in the original, has often been told. It shows a fruitful encounter of the scholars of Baghdâd with Plato, Aristotle, and Galen. But it is fundamentally unrelated to the more pedestrian Greek elements that were at the heart of Near Eastern Hellenism at the time of the Prophet. The Arabic translations from Greek made in Baghdâd were works of scholarship from ancient times that transmuted the glories of classical Greece into terms that scholarly Arabs could comprehend. This was a very different thing from the living Hellenism, treated here, of Nessana or 'Amra.

I have often asked myself how it must have felt to have lived through the Islamic conquest with all the accumulated baggage of the Hellenic-Semitic East, both Christian and pagan. How different would one have felt looking back? How would the passage of time have affected one's view of the past and one's sense of continuity with it? As in all great transitions in human history, it is unlikely that anyone realized then the importance of what was happening. That comes later. But if one lives long enough, one can see the whole process—what was there before and what was there after.

To acquire such perspective, one must look at the events from a great

---

27. Cf. R. Walzer, *Greek into Arabic* (Harvard, 1962), pp. 116–19. Of the major studies of Ḥunain, see for example G. Bergsträsser, *Ḥunain ibn Isḥâq. Über die syrischen und arabischen Galenübersetzungen* (Leipzig, 1925).

height. The scribe who wrote the accounts at Nessana in the days of ʿAbd al-Malik must have felt somewhat like Marcel Proust when he reached the end of his masterwork, *A la recherche du temps perdu*:

> There came over me a feeling of profound fatigue at the realization that all this long stretch of time not only had been uninterruptedly lived, thought, secreted by me, that it was my life, my very self, but also that I must, every minute of my life, keep it close by me, that it upheld me, that I was perched on its dizzying summit, that I could not move without carrying it about with me.
>
> My head swam to see so many years below me, and yet within me, as if I were thousands of leagues in height.
>
> I now understand why it was that the Duc de Guermantes whom, as I looked at him sitting in a chair, I marvelled to find shewing his age so little, although he had so many more years than I beneath him, as soon as he rose and tried to stand erect, had tottered on trembling limbs (like those of aged archbishops who have nothing solid on them except their metallic cross, with the young divinity students flocking assiduously about them) and had wavered as he made his way along the difficult summit of his eighty-three years, as if men were perched on giant stilts, sometimes taller than church spires, constantly growing and finally rendering their progress so difficult and perilous that they suddenly fall.
>
> I would therein describe men—even should that give them the semblance of monstrous creatures—as occupying in time a place far more considerable than the so restricted one allotted them in space, a place, on the contrary, extending boundlessly since, giant-like, reaching far back into the years, they touch simultaneously epochs of their lives—with countless intervening days between—so widely separated from one another in time.

High on those Proustian stilts at a dizzying elevation over the vast panorama of the past, one can see the whole flowing stream of historical change from one end to the other. An old man at Nessana, some Arab Duc de Guermantes whose life may be imagined to have spanned most of the seventh century, could have looked down upon the many separated epochs through which he had lived, so as to apprehend them all together, only with the aid of the powerful lens of Hellenism.

PLATES

Plate 1. New Paphos: Dionysus mosaic. Judgment of Marsyas. (Photo courtesy of V. Karageorghis.) Text pp. 5, 49–52.

Plate 2. New Paphos: Dionysus mosaic. Baby Dionysus in the lap of Hermes. (Photo courtesy of V. Karageorghis.) Text pp. 5, 49–52.

Plate 3. New Paphos: Dionysus mosaic. The victory of Cassiopeia. (Photo courtesy of V. Karageorghis.) Text pp. 5, 49–52.

Plate 4. New Paphos: Dionysus mosaic. Pendant to the victory of Cassiopeia. (Photo courtesy of V. Karageorghis.) Text pp. 5, 49–52.

Plate 5. Nabataean coin: *SNG* Amer. Num. Soc., Part 6, no. 1440 (Bostra). (Photo courtesy of American Numismatic Society.) Text pp. 8–9.

Plate 6. Dusares on a coin of Caracalla: *SNG* Amer. Num. Soc., Part 6, no. 1206 (Bostra). (Photo courtesy of American Numismatic Society.) Text pp. 8–9.

Plate 7. Dusares (aniconic) and motab on a coin of Elagabalus: *SNG* Amer. Num. Soc., Part 6, no. 1215 (Bostra). (Photo courtesy of American Numismatic Society.) Text pp. 8–9.

Plate 8. Dusares, apparently both aniconic and anthropomorphic, with motab on a coin of Elagabalus: Glendinning auction catalogue of March 10, 1965, no. 180 (Characmoba). Other specimens in M. Rosenberger, *The Coinage of Eastern Palestine* (1978), p. 22, Characmoba no. 2; A. Spijkerman, *The Coins of the Decapolis and Provincia Arabia* (1978), pp. 110–11, no. 5; *BMC Cat. Arabia*, p. 27, no. 3. Text pp. 8–9.

Plate 9. Sepphoris: Dionysus mosaic near the theater. (Photo courtesy of Eric Meyers.) Text pp. 48–49.

Plate 10. Abegg Stiftung: Dionysus hanging (left). (Photo courtesy of the foundation.) Text pp. 52–53.

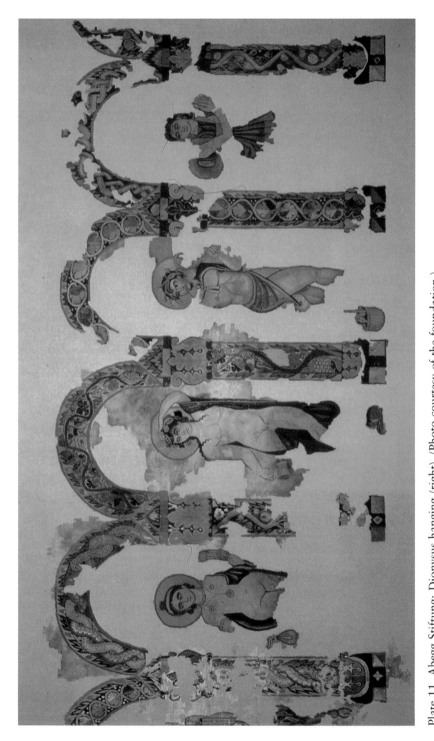

Plate 11. Abegg Stiftung: Dionysus hanging (right). (Photo courtesy of the foundation.) Text pp. 52–53.

Plate 12. Qaryat al-Faw: Painting of local benefactor (left). (Photo from A. Al-Anṣary, *Qaryat al-Faw* [1981], p. 136.) Text p. 75.

Plate 13. Qaryat al-Faw: Painting of local benefactor (right) with the name Zaki.
(Photo from A. Al-Anṣary, *Qaryat al-Faw* [1981], p. 137.) Text p. 75.

Plate 14. Qaryat al-Faw: Statue of Harpocrates. (Photo from A. Al-Anṣary, *Qaryat al-Faw* [1981], p. 104.) Text p. 75.

Plate 15. Qasr al-ʿAmra: Painting (perhaps baby Dionysus). Text pp. 78–80.

Plate 16. Umm er-Reşâş: Mosaic at Church of St. Stephen. (Photo from M. Piccirillo, *Liber Annuus* 37 [1987], pl. 8.) Text p. 80.

Index of Written Sources

Greek Literary Texts

Nonnos *Dionysiaca* 5.565–71: 26
            6.155–68: 26
            10.175–12:291: *44*
            12.171: *44*
            26.238: *62*
            40.311–23: *46*
            40.354–60: *46*
            40.363: *48*
            40.369: *47*
            40.429–35: *47*
            40.542–73: *48*
Nonnosus, *FHG* Müller 4:179–80: *73*
Pausanias 10.32.3: *19*
Perfect Discourse, see Latin versions in *Corpus Hermeticum, Asclepius*
Plato *Resp.* 327a: *32*
Porphyry *Life of Plotinus*: *35*
Proclus *Comm. in Plat. Cratylum* 5.55.5: *41*
Procopius *Wars* 1.17.11–12: *3*
Pseud.-Callisthenes 1.33.2: *23*
Pseud.-Plato I *Alc.* 133c: *36*
Shepherd of Hermas 10.1.4: *11*
Steph. Byz. s.v. Τύρος: *47*
Strabo 16.3.4, 766C: *47*
Suda s.v. Heraiscus: *25*
      Epiphanius: *25*
Tabula Cebetis 5.3: *52*
Theophrastus *de causis plant.* 2.5.5: *47*
         Hist. plant. 4.7.7: *47*

Latin Literary Texts

Ammianus Marcellinus 22.10.7: *11*
                22.16.12: *22*
                25.4.20: *11*
Codex Theodosianus 13.3.5: *11*
Corpus Hermeticum, Asclepius 2.327 Nock-Festugière: *58–60*
Macrobius *Sat.* 1.18.15: *41*

Syriac Literary Texts

Bardaişân *Book of the Laws of Countries* Nau: *31*
                              p. 1: *32*
                              p. 19: *13*
Brock, S., *Orientalia Lovanensia Periodica* 14 (1983): 203–46: *36*
Ephraem *de Fide*, CSCO 154:7: *34*
               154:268: *34*
Isaac of Antioch *Homiliae* Bedjan, p. 675: *35*
Jacob of Serûg "On the Fall of the Idols," *ZDMG* 29 (1875), 107–47: *37*
          "On the Spectacles of the Theatre," *Le Muséon* 48 (1935), 87–112: *37*
John of Ephesus *Hist. Eccles.* 3.3.27: *36*
                   3.3.28: *36, 38*
                   3.3.36: *1*

P. Gr. Rainer 19813, "Oracle of the Potter," *ZPE* 2 (1968), 204–7: *55–56*

Società Italiana: Pubblicazioni: Papiri greci e latini 7 (1925): 845, in Heitsch, *Griechische Dichterfragmente der römischen Kaiserzeit*, pp. 125–26: *61*

P. Gr. Vindob. 29788A-C, in Pamprepius, *Carmina* Livrea: *61*

Numismatics

BMC Cat. Alexandria, no. 1004: *23*
BMC Cat. Arabia, p. 27, no. 3: *9*
Coinage of Eastern Palestine, M. Rosenberger, Characmoba no. 2: *9*
Coins of the Decapolis and Provincia Arabia, A. Spijkerman, pp. 110–11, no. 5: *9*
Liber Annuus 34 (1984): 353–56 (coins of Arsapolis): *18*
SNG, ANS, 6 no. 1206: *9*
                    1215: *8*
                    1253: *8*
                    1440: *9*

General Index